BUFFALO GIRL COOKS BISON

BUFFALO GIRL COOKS
BISON
JENNIFER BAIN

TouchWood
Editions

TouchWood Editions
touchwoodeditions.com

LIBRARY AND ARCHIVES CANADA CATALOGUING IN PUBLICATION
Bain, Jennifer, author
Buffalo girl cooks bison / Jennifer Bain.

Includes index.
Issued in print and electronic formats.
ISBN 978-1-77151-075-2

1. Cooking (Buffalo meat). I. Title.

TX749.5.B84B33 2014   641.6'6292   C2014-901779-0

Edited by Cailey Cavallin
Proofread by Grace Yaginuma
Designed by Pete Kohut
Food styling by Noah Witenoff
Prop styling by Madeleine Johari
Food photography by Ryan Szulc
Remaining interior photos by Jennifer Bain, except as follows:
pages ii–iii, 224 (bottom), Rick MacKenzie;
pages xii, 7, 10, 22, 38, 73, 239, Kim Wright

Canadian   Patrimoine
Heritage   canadien

We gratefully acknowledge the financial support for our publishing activities from
the Canada Book Fund and the British Columbia Book Publishing Tax Credit.

This book was produced using FSC®-certified, acid-free papers,
processed chlorine free, and printed with soya-based inks.

1 2 3 4 5 18 17 16 15 14

PRINTED IN CHINA

To the Bain-MacKenzie clan and "the buffs"

Contents

Chapter 1
Ground (Burgers + Balls)

Chapter 4
Roasts

Chapter 5
Ribs/Shanks

Chapter 6
Sausages

At Home on My Range

We called him Blue Tag 741, for lack of a more personalized name. He was the first bison on our ranch in Alberta that I watched move from field to corral, then slaughter to freezer, and finally stove to stomach.

Blue Tag 741—blue for boy, 741 denoting the year he was born (2007) and his number (41)—was delicious in every way imaginable. His boneless blade roast became pot roast with chipotle-tomato sauce. His brisket was braised with pomegranate juice. His ground meat inspired endless burger and meatball experiments. Stewing meat was put to good use with Frito pie and wheat berry chili. Short ribs were braised with garlic and soy, dusted with ancho chili powder, slow-cooked with Guinness. When I didn't feel like "cooking," there were steaks—top sirloin, striploin, rib, tenderloin, skirt, flat iron (we love them all)—panfried in a cast-iron skillet, usually with kosher salt and freshly ground black pepper, smoked paprika mayo on the side.

I'll spare you the offal details (tail, liver, heart, tongue, and, yes, testicles) except to say that meaty shanks, and femurs split and broiled for marrow are treasures that should never be discarded.

Blue Tag's skull deteriorated naturally on a shed roof at our ranch. His hide was sent to a taxidermist. We ate most of his steaks, ribs, roasts, and odd bits ourselves, although our neighbors bought most of the jerky, sausages, and pepperoni made from his meat. It cost $1,428.63 to have Blue Tag slaughtered, cut, and wrapped at a small abattoir about an hour away from our southern Alberta ranch. I got to watch.

Blue Tag taught me a lot about ethical carnivorism—about meeting what you eat, caring enough to know how an animal is raised, and being respectful enough to eat every available part.

My Blue Tag 741 experience unfolded over 2008 and 2009, when I left my big-city food-writing job on maternity leave to play housewife/bison cook to my rancher husband. I fell hard for an iconic animal that has been brought back from near extinction by people eager to eat it. Now I'm on a mission to convince everyone to love North America's original red meat as much as I do.

Bison is a lean, wildly delicious alternative red meat that comes from heritage animals that are humanely raised and no longer endangered. You can raise bison, but you can't domesticate them. They're wild. They breed naturally. As ranchers like to say, you can lead a bison anywhere it wants to go.

Bison bison is the species name for the majestic herbivore with the shaggy brown coat and impressive hump. Buffalo is the romantic name, and the one my husband prefers. It confuses the heck out of most people, who think they're two different animals. Bison, part of the bovine family along with domestic cattle, are related to the European bison (also known as *wisent*). Dibs on the name *buffalo* also belong to the African Cape buffalo and the Asian water buffalo, which are different animals from our plains bison.

The nomenclature confusion dates back several centuries to the time when French explorers in North America referred to the animals as "les bœufs," as in oxen or cattle. English settlers changed that to "la buff." The nickname evolved from there into "buffalo."

The Canadian Bison Association (CBA) and the National Bison Association (NBA) in the United States want producers to help spread the word to consumers that "bison is indeed the American buffalo they know and love." Or so the associations say officially. During a chat, NBA executive director Dave Carter admitted, "I don't care what you call it as long as you eat it and enjoy it."

Like most people, I take the bilingual approach and switch easily between the terms. I favor buffalo for the animal and bison for the meat. When I'm writing about First Nations people, who always say buffalo, I follow their lead.

I now live and work in Toronto, Ontario, and holiday at the ranch. Rick, my husband, works at the ranch and spends his holidays in Toronto. He always comes bearing suitcases full of meat. We own a lot of freezers.

At work, I write a food column called "Saucy Lady." At the ranch, I'm the "Buffalo Girl." For this adventure cookbook, I hit the road to meet a bunch of buffalo people (or should I say bison people?), and I talked to others by phone.

This is our story. This is our food.

People always ask how a big-city journalist married a small-town rancher. Our mutual friend Adrienne set us up.

See, Rick is something of a city-slicker rancher. He grew up on a sheep/cattle ranch, but his parents, Ken and Margaret, encouraged Rick and his brothers, Colin and Norm, to pursue their own dreams. For Rick, that meant studying theater in Lethbridge and film in Toronto. He stayed in the city to indulge in his passions for music, film, art, coffee shops, and bakeries.

Me? I was born and raised in Toronto, studied journalism, and then wrote my way around Canada and Hong Kong before landing back in my hometown. I now write about food for the biggest newspaper in Canada and write cookbooks for fun.

When Rick and I met, we bonded over food. Here was a man who could bake a perfect apple pie and had a bison ranch. Rick kept an apartment in Toronto and commuted between worlds, learning to deal with the humped and horned herbivores that his brother Norm had introduced to the ranch in the 1990s. (The introduction of bison meant they could no longer raise sheep, because sheep can carry a disease that kills bison, so they don't mix. Rick still pines for lambs, his first animal love.)

Rick likes how bison are independent and don't need the intensive daily handling that other farm animals demand. They live outdoors and plow through the snow for food. Newborn calves stand within minutes and run within hours. We don't vaccinate our animals nor do we ever give them antibiotics.

Even if bison are hands-off animals, running a ranch is still a big job—there are wheat and field-pea crops to plant and harvest, and there's always a fence to fix at MacKenzie Ranch.

Oh, give me a home where the buffalo roam,
Where the deer and the antelope play . . .

Who doesn't know this American poem-turned-song? I hummed it as a kid. I live it as an adult.

MacKenzie Ranch is 12,000 acres (4,860 hectares) of bucolic Great Plains and short-grass prairie. But it's not all flat, like you'd imagine. There are broad, sometimes steep,

eroded valleys called coulees, which were likely formed when the last glaciers retreated. The ranch is split into two properties. The main section, where we live in Rick's childhood bungalow, is in the Chin Coulee. The other half of the land is about 15 minutes down the road on the shores of Kings Lake in the Etzikom Coulee.

We have enough bison, white-tailed deer, mule deer, and antelope (technically prong-horns) to bring to life "Home on the Range." We also have hawks, owls, cottontail rabbits, badgers, porcupines, coyotes (called *ky-oats* around here), rattlesnakes (which scare me to death), and Richardson's ground squirrels, commonly known as gophers.

The ranch is a 10-minute drive from Foremost, a village of 550 that celebrated its centennial in 2013. It has a school, grocery store, library, community center, and community hall. The grocery store covers the basics, but I have to make a two-hour round-trip drive to the city for things like cilantro, red curry paste, and quinoa. There are also churches and businesses, one Chinese restaurant, one bar, one golf course (with a clubhouse restaurant that offers a small menu), and a restaurant that's often between owners.

Rick's Scottish grandfather Murdo settled in the area in 1904 and grew his herd of sheep to 5,000. Rick's parents took over the ranch in 1951 and slowly converted it to cattle. His brother Norm took over in 1992 and switched things to bison. When Norm died in a car accident in 2003, Rick took charge of the ranch and has been running things ever since.

At the ranch, my food writer mantra of "meet what you eat" has become my daily reality.

I watch newborn bison frolic with their moms. I drive bison to slaughter. I respectfully eat every part of the bison that winds up in my freezer. I put the bison heads outside to decompose and bleach in the sun. I have created a garden of bones.

I'm still learning the lingo that goes with ranching. Female bison are called heifers when they're young and cows once they've given birth. Males are always called bulls. Frankly, it's easier to just call them "the girls" and "the boys."

I used to sit in a lawn chair in front of the corral willing the curious but skittish animals to befriend me, wanting to pat them as if they were cows or horses. It didn't happen. Our bison are wild. I've learned to respect that.

Bison are survivors.

There used to be 60 million of them roaming North America from Alaska to northern Mexico, and from coast to coast. For thousands of years, Aboriginal peoples relied on them for meat, shelter, clothing, tools, fuel, and utensils. As Europeans settled the West, they hunted the bison almost to extinction—for fur, meat, and bones, for sport, and to destroy the Native Americans.

By 1900, barely 1,000 bison remained. Luckily, conservationists and ranchers stepped in on both sides of the border, keeping herds privately and in national parks. In the 1990s, according to the CBA, the new livestock industry for bison really took off as consumers started hungering for this heritage food.

Today, the United States boasts almost 200,000 bison in private herds across every state. There are another 20,000 in public herds in parks, refuges, and wildlife management areas, and 15,000 in tribal herds. The 2011 Canadian Census of Agriculture showed 125,142 bison living on 1,211 farms, mainly in Alberta, Saskatchewan, and Manitoba, with some in British Columbia, Ontario, and Quebec. These are mainly plains bison. Canada also has more than 10,000 wood bison (an endangered relative of the plains bison) in public herds.

Bison is a niche industry that will never catch up to beef. Nobody wants it to. The United States slaughters about 60,000 bison per year for meat, Canada about 12,000. The average Canadian herd has just 103 bison.

Bison are treated as livestock (just like cattle) everywhere in Canada except British Columbia, where they are considered wildlife and regulated by the Ministry of the Environment. The rules in BC make it tough for herds to expand.

Bison is a naturally lean meat with virtually no marbling. It has less fat and fewer calories than rival meats, plus more protein and iron. It's high in omega-3 essential fatty acids. I haven't done my own nutritional testing, but I'll tell you what the Colorado-based National Bison Association says. It reports, in widely circulated statistics, that bison has 2.42 grams of fat, 28.44 grams of protein, 3.42 milligrams of iron, and 143 calories per 100 gram (3.5 ounce) serving of cooked meat. Compare that to USDA Choice beef (roughly equivalent to Canada's AAA): the same portion of cooked beef would provide 18.54 grams of fat, 27.21 grams of protein, 2.72 milligrams of iron, and 283 calories.

What I love—more than the nutritional stats—is the taste. I was raised on beef and adored prime rib dinners and well-marbled rib-eye steaks. To be honest, I probably craved the fat more than the meat. When I switched to bison, I missed the fat at first. Now I'm addicted to the intense meatiness. And I feel good about how our bison live and die.

Bison are wild.

Calves are born in the pasture each spring and stay with their moms until they're weaned, either in the fall or the next spring. The whole herd is baited into the corral with treats (legume-based pellets) when they must be sorted and tagged. The moms and girls (cows and heifers) are then sent back to the fields, along with any late calves, to live with the breeding bulls.

The heaviest males (bulls) are kept in two corrals and fed hay until they reach a slaughter weight of about 1,200 pounds (540 kilograms). There are usually about 40 of them in our herd, but the number ebbs and flows depending on prices, demand, and feed supplies.

We have about 200 bison. Half live on the Chin Coulee part of the ranch, where we live. The other half live down the road on the Etzikom Coulee part of the ranch.

I wish our bison were slaughtered in the field. Mobile abattoirs are starting to take hold in the United States, and many people feel it's more humane to spare the animals the journey to the abattoir. In Alberta, you can only use this option if you're keeping the meat for yourself. For now, most of our bison are driven several hours away, to a company that is licensed to slaughter and ship meat to Europe. We also take about five bison per year to a provincially licensed abattoir about an hour away. We can only sell this meat within Alberta. This is the meat that we eat, and that we use for freezer sales.

Eat it to save it. And eat it we do.

World leaders eat bison. When US president Barack Obama made his first visit to Parliament Hill, Canadian prime minister Stephen Harper served applewood-smoked plains bison.

Chefs eat it—and serve it at restaurants across North America. You'll meet a bunch of them throughout this cookbook, as they've generously shared recipes.

Average Americans eat it, thanks to billionaire media mogul Ted Turner. He has the world's largest private bison herd and cofounded Ted's Montana Grill, an upscale chain that has done more to popularize bison than any other restaurant in North America.

Slow Food members eat it. Plains bison is on the Slow Food Canada and Slow Food USA Ark of Taste, signifying that it's a delicious food that should be raised as naturally as possible, promoted, and eaten.

What other kinds of mere mortals eat bison? Locavores who build relationships with farmers. Ethical carnivores who shun factory-farmed meat. Eco-conscious eaters who make sustainable food choices. Red meat lovers seeking "steak without guilt." Food lovers who simply love the taste.

That's why this cookbook is vitally important. When people pay a premium for any-thing—be it a single-estate, cold-pressed extra-virgin olive oil or naturally raised bison from a small herd—it's crucial that they handle it properly.

As the NBA's Dave Carter stresses: "We've got to make that good first impression."

So let's get to it.

How to Cook Bison

Bison are lean, mean meat machines. Don't let the shaggy hair, big shoulders, and dramatic hump fool you. When you take away all of that, bison meat cuts can be smaller than beef cuts. They're definitely leaner because the meat doesn't usually marble. Marbling slows down the cooking process since the heat must penetrate the fat before it gets to the meat. The result is that bison cooks faster than beef. Be gentle and you'll be fine. And don't worry—the meat doesn't taste wild or gamy. It is slightly sweet, rich, and very flavorful.

People brag that bison is a hearty, dense meat, which is true. They also say you should be satisfied with a smaller portion than you would of other meats, but I'm still guilty of overeating.

I've divided this cookbook into chapters based on meat cuts. At the start of each, I've provided a cooking primer.

You may never have noticed this, but there's no consensus on what constitutes rare, medium-rare, and medium. Chefs say one thing, the United States government another, and the Canadian government yet another. Throw in the temperatures programmed into meat thermometers and you'll be totally confused.

For ground meat, I've gone with the conservative Canadian and US government guideline of cooking to 160°F (71°C). For steaks and roasts, I've veered closer to the temperatures used by chefs, who are careful not to waste money on overcooked food.

I love the laminated, four-color meat temperature fridge magnet from AmazingRibs.com. It details both chef and USDA recommendations, and provides color photos of the different stages of doneness for beef. Barbecue guru "Meathead" Goldwyn won the National Barbecue Association's Best BBQ Tool award for it in 2012. You can print it free from the website, or click on the link they provide to buy the magnet from Amazon.com for about six dollars (so the website will get a small referral fee).

"Cooking without a thermometer is like driving without a speedometer," Meathead likes to say. I agree wholeheartedly. You need a thermometer to cook meat properly. It's a small investment (usually $20 to $30, though of course you can spend a lot more) with a huge payoff. If you don't have a thermometer, do yourself a favor and buy one. It will take the guesswork out of cooking.

For roasts, I swear by the digital stainless steel programmable thermometer probes with long ovenproof wire cords. Just set the desired temperature for your meat and an alarm will go off when it's done. You don't even have to open the oven. (If you want to go old school and open the oven, a standard ovenproof meat thermometer is better than nothing.)

Standard cooking times based on weight (the old "cook for 10 minutes per pound" method) just aren't accurate. There's too much variation in the size, shape, and tenderness of roasts and steaks. You may have a 1-pound (450-gram) steak, but a smaller steak that's 2 inches (5 centimeters) thick will need more time to cook than a larger, thinner steak that's 1 inch (2.5 centimeters) thick. Besides, not everyone realizes this, but ovens are notoriously inaccurate. Some run hot, others run cold. Your 400°F (200°C) might be my 415°F (210°C) and my friend's 385°F (195°C). Consider buying a good oven thermometer as well.

Whether you bring meat to room temperature or cook it cold from the fridge will also have an impact on cooking time. So will the type, quality, and temperature of your skillet or roasting pan. For example, a room-temperature steak cooked in a searing hot cast-iron skillet will obviously cook much quicker than a cold steak in a nonstick skillet that has only been preheated for a few minutes.

It's controversial, but I like to bring my steaks to room temperature for 30 minutes to 1 hour before cooking to promote faster, more even cooking. On this point, however, I'm flexible. Some people swear this trick is an old wives' tale. If you prefer to cook your meat straight from the fridge, don't let me stop you.

How to Use These Recipes

This book contains 106 bison recipes and 23 "sides," which range from sauces and pickles to cooked veg and chutneys. The sides follow their original dishes, so you don't have to flip to another chapter to find them. But they can easily be mixed and matched with other recipes. Here's an example—Bison Steaks with Chimichurri Sauce are on page 86, but you can make the chimichurri and eat it with the Bison Puffs on page 54 or the CHARCUT Roast House's Bison Heart on page 204.

You don't have to make every element of a dish. The New Mexico Bison Burgers on page 30 showcase the decadence of an American restaurant burger and make you appreciate the prices you pay to dine out. I made the whole shebang once. Now I prefer to just make the cheeseburgers and tomato jam and use roasted chilies from a jar. I make the guacamole on its own. Sometimes I make roasted chilies to eat with the Cast-Iron Skillet Bison Steak on page 82. Remember, a recipe is just a starting point.

My Cooking Idiosyncrasies

Salt is such a touchy subject. I swear by kosher salt because it's coarse, easy to pinch, not too salty, and doesn't have any additives. Please don't use table salt, which has smaller grains (and anticaking additives), or you'll end up with a salty mess. People accuse me of undersalting my food, but salt is a very personal thing. Feel free to ignore my salt instructions, and "salt to taste" or "don't salt at all" if you prefer.

Pepper, on the other hand, is often a wasted opportunity. Don't buy the lame ground stuff. Grind your own. It's a small thing that makes a big difference. A few of my recipes call for "cracked pepper" when I want more texture and bite. I don't mind if you buy cracked pepper, but you can easily crack whole peppercorns in a mortar using a pestle.

I buy unsalted butter so I can control the amount of salt in a dish.

I use extra-virgin olive oil for most of my cooking. I don't have a problem with it smoking because I oil my steaks, not my hot skillets. I buy inexpensive bottles for cooking and more expensive bottles for finishing dishes and drizzling on salads.

"Chili powder" drives me crazy. Unbeknownst to most people, the stuff labeled chili powder in your supermarket spice aisle is probably a blend of chili peppers, cumin, coriander, salt, oregano, garlic powder, and cloves. I think of it as "chili con carne powder" because my mom put it in chili. I use a variety of chili powders in my cooking and try to specify when I want a pure blend, such as ancho or chipotle, two smoky offerings that are now widely available in supermarkets.

Finally, I created and/or tested all of the recipes in this book, adapting them, streamlining them, and even renaming them to suit my taste. I used our meat, from MacKenzie Ranching Co., for the recipe testing and the photographs.

Where to Buy Bison

Look for fresh and frozen bison in butcher shops that source local, sustainable, ethically raised meat. Farmers' markets and natural food stores are other good bets for bison, usually sold frozen. It's even in some supermarket chains.

The Canadian Bison Association website (canadianbison.ca) has a Where to Buy page that will connect you with farmers, wholesalers, farmers' markets, restaurants, and retail outlets. The National Bison Association website (bisoncentral.com) also has a Where to Buy Bison page. As well, they offer a free app called BisonFinder. The Bison Council has a searchable Find Bison database at thebisoncouncil.com. It includes US and Canadian listings.

Big retailers, including Costco, may stock bison—especially burgers and ground meat.

Various ranches and companies will ship frozen bison to your door.

FAMILY FRIEND AMY BODMAN JOINS RICK, CHARLIE, AND HAZEL ON A "BUFFALO SAFARI" AT MACKENZIE RANCH

Buy directly from a rancher and save a bundle. You can often buy a whole, half, or quarter animal and have it cut and processed exactly as you like. Or you can buy the parts you like in bulk. We have one customer who snaps up eye-of-round roasts, another who loves whole tenderloins, several who stockpile ground meat, and one who's crazy for jerky while his parents gravitate toward sausages.

CHAPTER 1

Ground (Burgers + Balls)

It's a cinch to cook ground meat. Just remember three things:

1. Cook until no pink remains.
2. Cook to 160°F if you're using a thermometer (preferably digital).
3. Ground bison doesn't shrink very much and isn't usually fatty, so you probably won't have to drain the cooked meat.

It takes years to finesse your perfect burger. This is mine. The small, loose patties and squishy white buns remind me of the burgers I grew up on, but the smashing technique is something I learned from three Toronto restaurants. My love of mustard-grilled patties comes from the secret menus at In-N-Out Burger in the United States and the Burger's Priest in Toronto. Secret sauce is, of course, a nod to the famous Big Mac sauce, the recipe for which is floating around the Internet. For an even simpler version, mix Thousand Island dressing with a little yellow mustard. If you love fried onions, make a double batch to have on hand for the week.

Mustard-Smashed Bison Cheeseburgers + Saucy Onions

Makes 4 burgers

Place the onions in a large nonstick skillet. Drizzle with the oil. Cook over medium-high heat, stirring, for 5 minutes. Reduce the heat to medium and continue cooking, stirring often, until the onions are nicely browned, about 25 minutes.

For the sauce, in a small bowl, stir together the mayonnaise, ketchup, relish, sugar, and vinegar. (Makes about ¼ cup.)

You can refrigerate the onions and sauce until needed. When you're ready to eat, put the onions and 2 tablespoons of sauce (or more/less to taste) in a small skillet and warm over medium heat. Or microwave until warm. Or stir together and serve cold.

For the burgers, heat a large cast-iron or heavy skillet (or the flat side of a cast-iron griddle if you have one) over medium for at least 15 minutes.

Divide the meat into 4 equal portions and gently form loose (not compacted) balls. Sprinkle the tops with salt. Squirt a generous dollop (about 2 teaspoons) of mustard on each ball. Place the balls 2 at a time in the hot skillet, mustard sides down. Cook undisturbed for 1 minute.

FRIED ONIONS:
2 onions (yellow, white, or red), chopped or halved and thinly sliced
2 Tbsp extra-virgin olive oil

SECRET SAUCE:
3 Tbsp mayonnaise
1 Tbsp ketchup
2 tsp sweet green relish
½ tsp granulated sugar
½ tsp white vinegar

CHEESEBURGERS:
1 lb ground bison
Kosher salt
Prepared yellow mustard
4 slices cheddar
4 small, soft white hamburger buns (such as Wonder), warmed in the microwave
4 slices tomato
4 small leaves green leaf lettuce
Ketchup

Using two metal spatulas, crisscrossed to give you leverage, quickly flatten each ball with a firm "smash" to form patties that are 4 inches in diameter and about ¾ inch thick. Cook for 2½ minutes. Carefully flip the burgers, using one of the spatulas to scrape up any crusty brown bits with the meat. Top each patty with a cheese slice. Cook until the burgers are no longer pink inside and their juices run clear, or until a digital thermometer reads 160°F, about 2 to 3 minutes.

Place 1 patty on the bottom half of each bun. Top each with saucy onions, tomato, lettuce, and ketchup (in that order). Cover with the top halves of the buns.

This is my all-time favorite "fancy" burger. It's from executive chef John Butler, who fills the cafeteria at St. Joseph's Health Centre (stjoe.on.ca) in Toronto with all kinds of glorious meals. When I visited for a story, he made these burgers. I loved them so much I put them in my first book, *Toronto Star Cookbook: More Than 150 Diverse and Delicious Recipes Celebrating Ontario* (Appetite by Random House, 2013). Here they are again. I can't get enough of them.

Bison Burgers with Smoked Gouda + Red Pepper Relish

Makes 6 burgers

In a large mixing bowl, whisk the egg and oil. Add the bison, bread crumbs, parsley, onion, garlic, chili, Dijon mustard, grainy mustard, and lemon zest. Mix thoroughly by hand, massaging the ingredients together. Divide into 6. Roll by hand into balls, and then flatten by hand into ¾-inch-thick patties. Place the burgers on a baking sheet and cover with plastic. Refrigerate for at least 1 hour to let them firm up.

Heat a lightly oiled large cast-iron skillet over medium-high. Add the burgers, in batches if needed, and cook for 5 minutes per side or to desired doneness. Top each burger with a cheese slice for the last minute of cooking. Burgers should be cooked to 160°F.

Alternately, heat the oven to 350°F. Sear the burgers for 1 minute per side in a lightly oiled ovenproof skillet, and then place the skillet in the oven and bake for 10 minutes or until the burgers are cooked to 160°F or to desired doneness, adding the cheese for the last minute of cooking.

Place 1 patty on the bottom half of each bun. If desired, top each with lettuce, tomato, and Red Pepper Relish to taste. Cover each with the top half of the bun.

1 large egg

1 Tbsp extra-virgin olive oil

1½ lb ground bison

¼ cup fresh bread crumbs

¼ cup chopped flat-leaf parsley

1 small red onion, finely diced

1 large clove garlic, minced

1 long red chili (about 4 inches), seeded and minced

1 Tbsp Dijon mustard

1 Tbsp grainy mustard

Finely grated zest from 1 lemon

6 thin slices smoked Gouda or other smoked cheese

6 buns, toasted or warmed if desired

6 leaves green leaf lettuce (optional)

6 slices tomato (optional)

Red Pepper Relish (optional, see p. 20)

I adore this easy relish from John Butler. It's perfect with bison burgers, but this makes a big batch, so use it lavishly wherever you like.

Red Pepper Relish

Makes about 4 cups

In a medium saucepan, combine the bell peppers, jalapenos, apples, cider vinegar, sugar, and salt. Bring to a boil over high heat. Reduce the heat to medium. Briskly simmer until thick and reduced to about 4 cups, about 35 to 45 minutes. Cool for 10 minutes. Stir in the cilantro. Refrigerate until cold before serving. This will keep for up to 2 weeks in the fridge.

5 red bell peppers, finely chopped

4 jalapenos, seeded and minced

2 tart apples (such as McIntosh or Northern Spy), peeled and chopped

1½ cups cider vinegar

1½ cups granulated sugar

1½ Tbsp kosher salt

¼ cup chopped cilantro

North American bison, Spanish smoked paprika, and Italian Gorgonzola are an inspired multicultural mashup. These burgers come from Maddy Kelly, president of Domicile Interiors (domicileinteriors.com) in Calgary. She designed the burgers during her gourmet catering days using Alberta-grown ingredients. She later shared the recipe with Carmen Creek Gourmet Bison for its website (carmencreek.com).

Smoked Paprika Bison Burgers

Makes 4 burgers

In a mixing bowl, combine the bison, egg, panko or regular bread crumbs, garlic, onion, Worcestershire sauce, paprika, salt, pepper, and cheese. Mix by hand. Shape into 4 patties, each about 4 inches wide and ½ inch thick. Refrigerate on a plate, covered, for at least 1 hour to help them firm up.

In a large nonstick skillet over medium-high, heat the oil. Add the meat patties and cook just until no longer pink inside, about 3 to 4 minutes per side. Burgers should be cooked to 160°F.

Sandwich the burgers in the buns.

1 lb ground bison

1 large egg

½ cup panko (Japanese bread crumbs) or dried bread crumbs

2 large cloves garlic, minced

¼ cup finely diced red onion

1 tsp Worcestershire sauce

1 Tbsp smoked paprika

½ tsp kosher salt

½ tsp freshly ground black pepper

5 oz diced Gorgonzola or other blue cheese

1 Tbsp canola oil

4 buns, toasted or warmed if desired

Mixing blueberries and bison—both native to North America—makes me feel like an early settler living off the land. Assertive rosemary provides a hint of the forest while brie provides creamy richness. I make these burgers spread with 1 tablespoon of soft, unripened goat cheese (chèvre) when I crave something tangier.

Blueberry + Brie Bison Burgers

Makes 4 burgers

In a mixing bowl, combine the bison, blueberries, panko or regular bread crumbs, and rosemary. Season with salt and pepper. Mix by hand. Shape into 4 patties, each about 4 inches wide and ½ inch thick. Refrigerate, covered, for at least 1 hour to help them firm up.

In a large nonstick skillet over medium-high, heat the oil. Add the burgers. Cook just until no longer pink inside, about 3 to 4 minutes per side, adding the cheese during the last minute of cooking. (If needed, cover the skillet briefly to help melt the cheese.) Burgers should be cooked to 160°F.

Sandwich the burgers in the buns.

1 lb ground bison

½ cup fresh or frozen and thawed blueberries

¼ cup panko (Japanese bread crumbs) or dried bread crumbs

3 Tbsp finely chopped fresh rosemary

Kosher salt

Freshly ground black pepper

1 Tbsp canola oil

4 thin slices brie

4 buns, toasted or warmed if desired

At DMK Burger Bar (dmkburgerbar.com) in Chicago, you can make any burger a bison burger. Owner Michael Kornick originally created this recipe as a summer offering using Michigan blueberries, but it has earned itself a permanent place on the menu. Michael shared these sliders at thebisoncouncil.com. This recipe also can be used to make regular-size burgers. Simply adjust the amount of cheese and toppings that you use.

Bison Sliders with Blueberry Barbecue Sauce, Goat Cheese + Marinated Red Onions

Makes 8 sliders

In a medium mixing bowl, combine the bison, garlic, and parsley. Season with salt and pepper. Mix well by hand and then divide the mixture into 8. Gently form into patties, each about 2½ inches in diameter. If time allows, refrigerate, covered, for at least 1 hour to let the patties firm up.

In a large nonstick skillet or grill pan over medium-high, heat the oil. Add the burgers. Cook just until no longer pink inside, about 3 minutes per side. Burgers should be cooked to 160°F. Alternately, heat the barbecue to medium-high and grease the grill. Place the burgers directly on the grill, cooking just until no longer pink inside, about 3 minutes per side.

To assemble, crumble or spread 1 tablespoon of chèvre on the bottom of each bun. Top each with a small portion of marinated onions and a burger. Top each burger with a generous dollop of barbecue sauce and more onions, if desired. Cover with bun tops.

1 lb ground bison

2 Tbsp minced garlic

¼ cup finely chopped flat-leaf parsley

Kosher salt

Freshly ground black pepper

1 Tbsp extra-virgin olive oil

8 Tbsp chèvre (fresh goat cheese), at room temperature, divided

8 slider buns (each about 2½ inches in diameter), toasted, grilled, or warmed

Marinated Red Onions (see p. 24)

Blueberry Barbecue Sauce (see p. 25)

Every chef knows that something tart and crunchy works well as a burger topping. This recipe is from Chicago restaurateur Michael Kornick via The Bison Council. If julienning, or cutting into matchsticks, is too finicky for you, just cut your onion in half and then slice as thinly as possible.

Marinated Red Onions

Makes about 1 cup

In a medium mixing bowl, whisk the red wine vinegar and sugar until the sugar is dissolved. Add the onion. Season to taste with salt and pepper. Let stand for 1 hour on the counter, or longer in the fridge, stirring occasionally. Strain before using. Refrigerate for up to 2 weeks.

1 cup red wine vinegar

1 Tbsp granulated sugar

1 small red onion, julienned or cut into thin matchsticks

Kosher salt

Freshly ground black pepper

" I've been serving bison for over a decade in my restaurant. Our customers have been so grateful for its flavor and texture and health benefits." —Michael Kornick

Michael is a founding ambassador for the council, which works to convince chefs and consumers to try bison. The other founding ambassadors are food writer/Meatopia (meatopia.org) founder Josh Ozersky and registered dietitian/TV show host/cookbook author Ellie Krieger.

This sauce, from Chicago restaurateur Michael Kornick via The Bison Council, packs a punch. It's assertively blueberry with hot, sweet, and tart notes. Save the leftovers for sandwiches and more burgers. For more recipes, visit thebisoncouncil.com.

Blueberry Barbecue Sauce

Makes about 1¼ cups

In a medium saucepan over medium-high, heat the oil. Add the onion and jalapeno. Cook, stirring, for 3 minutes. Add the brown sugar, ketchup, mustard, rice wine vinegar, and hot sauce. Bring to a simmer, stirring. Add the blueberries. Cook, stirring often, for 5 minutes. Remove from the heat and let cool to room temperature for about 1 hour.

In a blender or food processor, purée the cooled sauce. Strain through a fine-mesh sieve, discarding the solids. (If seeds don't bother you, skip this step.) Refrigerate the sauce, covered, until ready to use.

1 Tbsp extra-virgin olive oil

¼ cup finely chopped onion, preferably Spanish or other sweet variety

1 Tbsp minced jalapeno

¼ cup light brown sugar

¼ cup ketchup

¼ cup Dijon mustard

¼ cup rice wine vinegar

1 tsp hot sauce

2 cups fresh or frozen blueberries

In Toronto, I live in an amazing, vibrant emerging neighborhood called the Pocket, which is just a few blocks away from Greektown. When I think of Greek food, I think of spinach, feta, and lamb. You won't find lamb in these burgers, but you will find the other two flavors. I'm thrilled that thick Greek yogurt has finally taken off so you no longer have to strain plain yogurt.

Greektown Bison Burgers

Makes 4 burgers

In a large mixing bowl, combine the bison, spinach, feta, and garlic. Season to taste with salt and pepper. Mix by hand. Form into 4 patties, each about 4 inches in diameter and ½ inch thick. Refrigerate, covered, for at least 1 hour to help them firm up.

In a large nonstick skillet over medium-high, heat the oil. Cook the burgers just until no longer pink inside, about 3 to 4 minutes per side. Burgers should be cooked to 160°F.

Meanwhile, for the tzatziki sauce, in a small bowl, stir together the yogurt, cucumber, and lemon juice. Season to taste with salt and pepper.

Place a burger on the bottom half of each bun. Add a dollop of tzatziki sauce to each, as desired. Cover with bun tops.

1 lb ground bison

½ cup chopped cooked spinach or baby spinach, squeezed dry

½ cup crumbled feta cheese

2 large cloves garlic, minced

Kosher salt

Freshly ground black pepper

1 Tbsp canola oil

4 buns, toasted or warmed if desired

QUICK TZATZIKI SAUCE:

½ cup plain Greek yogurt

¼ cup peeled and finely diced English cucumber

1 Tbsp fresh lemon juice

Kosher salt

Freshly ground black pepper

Kevin D. Birch, executive chef of the Rogers Centre (home of the Toronto Blue Jays), shared recipes for two condiments along with a superb burger (which he urges you to barbecue over charcoal). He says these burgers "deserve an aged white Canadian maple cheddar or at the very least a nice aged white cheddar, three years old or more." Kevin fell in love with bison while working at the Fairmont Banff Springs Resort.

Maple-Whisky Bison Burgers with Mustard or Chutney

Makes 6 burgers

In a medium nonstick skillet over medium-high heat, melt the butter. Add the onions, whisky, and maple syrup. Cook, stirring, until the onions are soft and golden, about 7 to 10 minutes. Refrigerate until cold.

In a mixing bowl, combine the onion mixture, bison, powdered mustard, Worcestershire sauce, pepper, and salt. Divide into 6 balls. Flatten into patties, each about 4 inches in diameter and ½ inch thick. Refrigerate, covered, for at least 1 hour before cooking to help them firm up.

Heat a large cast-iron skillet over medium for at least 15 minutes. Cook the burgers, in two batches, to 160°F, about 3 to 4 minutes per side. Add the cheese during the last minute of cooking.

Sandwich the burgers in the buns, topped with Saskatoon Berry + Honey Mustard or Saskatoon Berry + Pear Chutney, if desired.

2 tsp unsalted butter

1 cup finely diced yellow onions

2 Tbsp Canadian whisky

2 Tbsp pure maple syrup

1½ lb ground bison

1 tsp powdered mustard

1 tsp Worcestershire sauce

1 tsp cracked black pepper

½ tsp kosher salt

6 thin slices aged white cheddar or maple cheddar

6 crusty rolls, such as ciabatta, or any hamburger buns

Saskatoon Berry + Honey Mustard (optional, see p. 28)

Saskatoon Berry + Pear Chutney (optional, see p. 29)

Here's the first of Toronto chef Kevin D. Birch's condiments. Saskatoon berries (aka serviceberries) are native to North America and abound in the Canadian Prairies. They may look like blueberries, but they have a unique, wild flavor and don't break down and release water like other berries. Their growing season is short so they're usually sold frozen. Look for them at pick-your-own spots, farmers' markets, and local food stores.

Saskatoon Berry + Honey Mustard

Makes about 1 cup

In a small bowl, combine the juice and mustard seeds. Refrigerate overnight. Add the honey, rice wine vinegar, and berries. Stir well. If you want smooth mustard, transfer to a blender and purée. Refrigerate, covered, overnight to let thicken.

½ cup cranberry or grape juice

¼ cup yellow mustard seeds

¼ cup honey

¼ cup unseasoned rice wine vinegar or Champagne vinegar

2 Tbsp fresh or frozen saskatoon berries or blueberries, or dried cranberries or blueberries

The flavors are richer and bolder than beef." —Kevin D. Birch

Another flavor-packed, bison-friendly condiment from Toronto chef Kevin D. Birch. Saskatoons are dense berries with low water content, so they don't break down and turn jammy the way blueberries do.

Saskatoon Berry + Pear Chutney

Makes about 2 cups

In a medium saucepan over medium-high heat, bring the rice wine vinegar and brown sugar to a boil. Boil for 2 minutes. Add the berries, pears, apple, jalapeno, bell pepper, onion, ginger, and garlic. Return to a boil. Reduce the heat to medium and simmer briskly, stirring often, until the mixture is thick and the consistency of jam, about 30 to 45 minutes. (You may need to adjust the heat up or down.) Stir in the rosemary. Season to taste with salt and pepper. Let cool. If too thick once cooled, add small amounts of water until desired consistency is achieved. Refrigerate in a sealed container for up to 3 weeks.

¼ cup unseasoned rice wine vinegar

½ cup lightly packed light brown sugar

1½ cups fresh or frozen saskatoon berries or blueberries

3 Bartlett pears, peeled and diced

½ apple (such as McIntosh or Granny Smith), peeled and diced

½ jalapeno, seeded and finely diced

¼ cup finely diced red bell pepper

2 Tbsp finely diced red onion

1½ Tbsp peeled and minced ginger

1½ tsp minced garlic

1 Tbsp finely chopped fresh rosemary

Kosher salt

Freshly ground black pepper

These hefty beauties hail from Ted's Montana Grill, the American chain of restaurants co-owned by media mogul/bison rancher Ted Turner and restaurateur George McKerrow Jr. Corporate chef Chris Raucci shared this recipe. There's a bit of work involved, but you don't have to use all of the components and can mix and match to suit your mood. Anaheim peppers are large, pale green, and sweet. You could substitute the darker green poblanos or even cubanelles. In a pinch, simply use green bell peppers or even roasted red peppers from a jar.

New Mexico Bison Burgers

Makes 4 burgers

Preheat the oven to 500°F. Place the peppers on a baking sheet and drizzle with the olive oil. Roast in the oven for 20 to 30 minutes, turning twice, until the skins are wrinkled and charred. Place the peppers in a mixing bowl and cover tightly with plastic wrap to let the peppers steam. Let stand for 30 minutes. Discard the stems. Cut each pepper in half. Discard the skins and seeds. You should have 4 large pieces of pepper.

Form the bison into 4 loose (never compacted) patties with rough edges. They should be about 5 to 6 inches in diameter. Place the patties on a large plate. Refrigerate for at least 1 hour to firm up.

Heat a nonstick grill pan over medium-high. Drizzle with the canola oil.

Place the spice mixture in a small bowl. Sprinkle one side of each burger with some of the spice. Place the burgers, seasoned sides down, in the pan. (You may have to do this in 2 batches.) Sprinkle the unseasoned sides with more of the spice mixture. Cook the burgers for 4 minutes. Gently flip them with a spatula, taking care not to press them down. Season the tops with a final sprinkling of spice mixture. Add the peppers to the pan, if there is room, so they will warm up and char slightly. Cook for 2 minutes. Divide the grated cheese or cheese slices among the burgers. Cover the pan with a big lid. Cook for 2 minutes or until the cheese has melted, the burgers' juices run clear, and the burgers reach 160°F.

Place the cheeseburgers on the bun bottoms. Top each with 1 piece of pepper and ¼ cup of guacamole. Spread 1 tablespoon of tomato jam on the inside of each bun top and then place them on the burgers.

2 Anaheim peppers

1 tsp extra-virgin olive oil

2 lb ground bison

1 Tbsp canola oil

About 2 tsp Ted Turner's Special Spice Mixture (see opposite page), or to taste, divided

6 oz pepper jack cheese, grated, or 4 slices Monterey jack cheese with jalapeno

4 kaiser rolls or other large hamburger buns, toasted

1 cup TMG Guacamole (see opposite page), divided

4 Tbsp TMG Spicy Tomato Jam (see p. 32), divided

Bison rancher Ted Turner shared this recipe for his favorite burger spice mixture with *The Martha Stewart Show* in 2006. It's definitely for salt lovers. Try to find a brand of seasoned salt that doesn't contain MSG.

Ted Turner's Special Spice Mixture

Makes 2 tablespoons

In a small bowl, stir together the kosher salt, garlic salt, seasoned salt, onion salt, and pepper. Store in a sealed container at room temperature for up to 3 months.

1½ tsp kosher salt

1½ tsp garlic salt

1 tsp seasoned salt

1 tsp onion salt

1 tsp freshly ground black pepper

This spicy guacamole offers a pleasing chunky texture instead of the usual smooth one, although that does make it more challenging to eat on burgers. If there's one thing that stands out from watching chefs cook, it's to use Roma (plum) tomatoes when field tomatoes aren't in season. Romas are firm and not too juicy, so they're easy to dice. The lime juice will keep the avocado from immediately browning, but try to eat this ASAP.

TMG Guacamole

Makes about 1¼ cups

In a medium bowl, combine the tomatoes, onion, lime juice, jalapeno, and salt. Stir well. Add the avocados and toss carefully.

¼ cup finely diced tomatoes

1 Tbsp finely diced white onion

Juice of 1 lime

1½ tsp minced jalapeno

Large pinch kosher salt

1½ Haas avocados, pitted, peeled, and diced

This was one of the last recipes I test-drove for this cookbook, and it has become one of my favorites. This smoky, spicy sauce (it's not a conventional sweet and sticky jam) is great slathered on a burger bun but works equally well on sandwiches or pasta.

TMG Spicy Tomato Jam

Makes about 1 cup

In a medium saucepan over medium-high, heat the oil. Add the onion. Cook, stirring, for 5 minutes. Add the garlic. Cook, stirring, for 1 minute. Add the tomatoes, brown sugar, red wine vinegar, chipotle purée, honey, tomato paste, oregano, cumin, and salt. Bring to a boil and then reduce the heat to medium. Simmer briskly, stirring often, for 15 minutes. As the mixture starts to thicken and reduce, you may need to turn the heat to medium-low. Let cool for 5 minutes.

Transfer the mixture to a food processor. Purée until smooth. Refrigerate, covered, for up to 2 weeks.

1 Tbsp canola oil

½ cup finely diced yellow onion

1½ Tbsp chopped garlic

1 cup canned diced tomatoes with liquid

¼ cup light brown sugar

¼ cup red wine vinegar

1 Tbsp puréed canned chipotle chilies packed in adobo sauce (see Cooking Tip)

1½ tsp honey

1½ tsp tomato paste

½ tsp dried oregano leaves

½ tsp ground cumin

½ tsp kosher salt

Cooking Tip: Chipotle peppers in adobo sauce are smoked and dried jalapenos packed in a spiced tomato sauce. They come in small cans. Dump the whole can in a food processor and purée the contents. Scoop the purée by the tablespoonful into an ice cube tray. When the cubes are frozen, pop them into a plastic bag and use as needed.

Toronto chef Ben Gundy came up with these decadent bison-pork burgers when he was on the Christine Cushing show *Fearless in the Kitchen*. He co-owns the butcher shop Olliffe (olliffe.ca). Any butcher who cuts pork chops should be able to sell you hard pork fat. Ben's brother, co-owner Sam Gundy, suggests upscale burger toppings like pickled jalapenos, roasted tomatoes, sautéed mushrooms, Manchego cheese, cured black olive aioli, and saffron aioli.

Olliffe's Chorizo-Spiced Bison Burgers

Makes 4 burgers

If you have a meat grinder, make sure it's chilled, and then run the bison meat and pork fat through it. Otherwise, in a food processor, combine the bison and pork fat. Pulse until coarsely chopped (be careful not to process too much or it will turn to mush). Transfer to a bowl. Add the prosciutto, garlic, parsley, paprika, chili powder, and pepper. Mix thoroughly by hand. Divide into 4. Form into patties, each about 5 inches in diameter. Refrigerate, covered, for at least 1 hour to help the burgers firm up.

Heat a greased barbecue or a nonstick grill pan over medium-high. Cook the burgers for 4 minutes per side. Burgers should be cooked to 160°F.

Sandwich the burgers in the buns.

1½ lb bison shoulder or blade meat, cut into ¾-inch dice

4 oz hard pork fat (leaf lard, kidney fat, or back/loin fat), cut into ¼-inch dice

4 oz prosciutto, finely diced

½ tsp minced garlic

1 Tbsp finely chopped flat-leaf parsley

1 Tbsp smoked paprika

2 tsp chili powder

1½ tsp freshly ground black pepper

4 buns, toasted or warmed if desired

At Afghan restaurants, you'll find a heavily spiced take on burgers called chaplee kebab. Ground beef is brought alive with freshly ground coriander seeds and red pepper flakes. The meat is shaped into patties (but called kebabs) and served alongside salad, basmati rice (sometimes studded with raisins and carrots), and naan (flatbread). The key is to grind the coriander seeds yourself so you get a rougher, more toothsome texture than with preground coriander. And to use bison, of course.

Afghan-Inspired Bison Patties

Makes 4 patties

In a small, dry skillet over medium heat, toast the coriander seeds until fragrant and starting to darken. Transfer the seeds to a coffee grinder dedicated to spices and roughly grind just until coarsely crushed. You can also use a mortar and pestle.

In a medium mixing bowl, combine the bison, coriander, and red pepper flakes. Mix by hand. Shape into 4 thin patties, each about 5 inches in diameter and ¼ inch thick. Refrigerate on a plate, covered, for at least 1 hour to help the patties firm up.

Lightly oil a large nonstick skillet and place it over medium-high heat. Cook the patties in the skillet, in batches if needed, just until no longer pink inside and the juices run clear, about 3 to 4 minutes per side. Burgers should be cooked to 160°F.

2 Tbsp coriander seeds
1 lb ground bison
1 Tbsp red pepper flakes
Canola oil, for greasing

When you get that jones for retro meatballs, bison comes through big time. I make my balls small so they cook fast. The key to the sauce is finding your perfect balance of sweet (sugar/ketchup) and sour (vinegar). This is mine—feel free to adjust it. No cocktail party planned? Serve these overtop of cooked spaghetti or steamed rice.

Sweet + Sour Bison Party Balls

Makes about 24 balls

Preheat the oven to 350°F. Grease a 13 × 9-inch glass baking dish.

For the meatballs, in a medium mixing bowl, combine the bison, panko or regular bread crumbs, onion, garlic, and pepper. Mix well by hand. By the heaping tablespoon, form into 1-inch balls. You should get 24. Transfer the meatballs to the baking dish.

Meanwhile, for the sauce, in a small saucepan combine the brown sugar, ketchup, vinegar, and ⅓ cup of the water. Bring to a boil over medium-high heat, whisking constantly.

In a small bowl, whisk the cornstarch with the remaining 2 tablespoons of water until smooth. Stir into the sauce. Cook, stirring constantly, for 1 minute to thicken.

Pour the sauce over the meatballs, turning to coat well. Bake for 20 minutes, turning once.

To serve, transfer the meatballs to a serving plate. If you like, insert a toothpick into each.

MEATBALLS:

1 lb ground bison

½ cup panko (Japanese bread crumbs) or dried bread crumbs

1 small yellow onion, finely chopped

2 large cloves garlic, minced

1 tsp freshly ground black pepper

SWEET + SOUR SAUCE:

½ cup lightly packed light brown sugar

½ cup ketchup

⅓ cup white vinegar

⅓ cup plus 2 Tbsp water, divided

1 Tbsp cornstarch

Chipotle and cilantro is probably my favorite flavor pairing. Here they modernize meatballs. Panko (coarse Japanese bread crumbs) replaces conventional dried bread crumbs, fragrant fresh cilantro replaces dried herbs, and chipotle chilies provide a smoky kick. Panko is common in the international aisle of most supermarkets. Enjoy these balls with a salad, or perch them on spaghetti.

Bison Balls with Chipotle + Cilantro

Makes about 12 balls (for 4 servings)

Preheat the oven to 450°F. Grease a 13 × 9-inch glass baking dish and set aside until needed.

In a food processor or blender, combine the tomatoes and their juices and the chipotle purée. Purée until smooth; set aside until needed.

In a mixing bowl, combine the bison, panko, cilantro, eggs, garlic, and salt. Mix by hand. Use a ¼-cup measure to scoop out portions of the mixture. Gently shape into about 12 balls.

Place the balls in the prepared baking dish, and bake for 15 minutes. Remove from the oven and turn the meatballs, and then cover with the tomato-chipotle sauce. Bake for 20 minutes, stirring in water if the sauce starts to dry out.

To serve, transfer the meatballs to a serving dish using tongs. If the sauce is too thick, stir in hot water to reach desired consistency. Pour the sauce over the balls.

1 (28 oz) can diced tomatoes

3 Tbsp puréed canned chipotle chilies packed in adobo sauce (see Cooking Tip, p. 32)

1½ lb ground bison

½ cup panko

½ cup chopped cilantro

2 large eggs

3 large cloves garlic, minced

1 tsp kosher salt

"Buffalo" Bob Wilson of Morning Star Bison Ranch on Vancouver Island near Nanaimo created these meatballs "with a Canadian twist" just for this cookbook. Buffalo Bob presides over tours of his 240-acre (97-hectare) ranch, making sure people safely view his 100 plains bison from a hay wagon ride or from behind a fence. He runs the small Yippy Ki'Yeah Café at the ranch and sells most of his meat as freezer packs, shipping within British Columbia from m-star.ca. Morning Star is North America's westernmost bison ranch.

Morning Star Bison Balls

Makes 12 balls

Preheat the oven to 350°F. Grease a 13 × 9-inch glass baking dish.

In a medium mixing bowl, combine the bison, oats, cheddar, and syrup. Mix well by hand. If the mixture seems dry and isn't holding together well, add more syrup, 1 tablespoon at a time. If the mixture seems wet, add more oats, 1 tablespoon at a time. Roll into 12 balls, each about 2 ounces.

Place the balls in the prepared dish. Bake for 30 minutes, turning once.

1 lb ground bison
½ cup steel-cut oats
½ cup grated old cheddar
¼ cup pure maple syrup

" Bison are a very intelligent and interesting animal and as I stand amongst them during winter feeding I see such a beautiful creature. My herd comes to me when I call them and my main alpha bull eats from my hand. We're like one big happy family. No stresses and relaxed." —"Buffalo" Bob Wilson

Toronto food and travel writer Habeeb Salloum, the son of Syrian homesteaders, didn't eat bison while growing up in Saskatchewan. But when he realized the majestic animal was making a comeback, he wrote *Bison Delights: Middle Eastern Cuisine, Western Style* (University of Regina Press, 2010). Habeeb calls this dish Shawrabat 'Adas, or Iraqi-Style Lentil Soup. I'm a tad greedy, so I've doubled the meatballs.

Red Lentil Soup with Mini Bison Meatballs

Makes 6 to 8 servings

In a large saucepan, combine the lentils and water. Bring to a boil over high heat. Reduce the heat to medium-low and cover. Cook until the lentils turn mushy and start to disintegrate, about 40 minutes.

Meanwhile, in a large nonstick skillet over medium, heat 2 tablespoons of the oil. Add the onion. Cook, stirring, until golden, about 10 minutes. Transfer to a bowl and set aside.

In a mixing bowl, combine the bison, garlic, 1 teaspoon of the salt, 1 teaspoon of the pepper, and 1 teaspoon of the coriander. Form the mixture by the teaspoonful into marble-size balls.

In the skillet used to cook the onion over medium-high, heat the remaining 2 tablespoons of oil. Add the meatballs. Cook, stirring or shaking the pan, until browned all over, about 8 minutes.

To the lentils in the saucepan, add the cooked onion, meatballs, remaining 1 teaspoon of salt, remaining 1 teaspoon of pepper, remaining ½ teaspoon of coriander, cumin, and turmeric. Cook over medium-low heat for 10 minutes. Stir in the lemon juice and serve.

1 cup dried split red lentils, rinsed

8 cups water

4 Tbsp canola oil, divided

1 large yellow onion, finely chopped

1 lb ground bison

4 cloves garlic, minced

2 tsp kosher salt, divided

2 tsp freshly ground black pepper, divided

1½ tsp ground coriander, divided

1 tsp ground cumin

½ tsp powdered turmeric

2 Tbsp fresh lemon juice

Josh Dockstator runs the Big Chief food truck in Hamilton (twitter.com/thebigchiefco). He grew up with a Welsh mom and an Iroquois dad, so his formative food years were a mishmash of bannock and roast beef dinners with Yorkshire pudding. His food truck offers "a contemporary twist on traditional First Nations cuisine." Josh mixes a pound of bison with a quarter pound of beef for added fat, but I've stuck with pure bison.

Bison Meatballs with Carrot Gravy + Wild Rice Pilaf

Makes 4 servings

Preheat the oven to 350°F.

In a medium mixing bowl, combine the bison, garlic, Italian seasoning, salt, and pepper. Mix thoroughly by hand. Form into 12 balls. Place the balls in a roasting pan with the carrots, celery, and onions. Cover with foil. Bake for 30 minutes. Remove the foil and bake for an additional 30 minutes. Transfer the meatballs to a plate. Cover and keep warm.

Transfer the vegetables and any pan drippings to a food processor. Add the stock and purée. If you want a finer purée, pass the mixture through a fine-mesh sieve to strain, discarding the solids. Place the carrot gravy into a small saucepan and set over medium heat, stirring occasionally.

In a small skillet over medium-high heat, whisk the butter and flour constantly until light brown. Whisk into the carrot gravy.

To serve, divide the wild rice pilaf among 4 plates. Top each with 3 meatballs. Drizzle each serving with carrot gravy. Garnish with cilantro, if desired.

1¼ lb ground bison

3 cloves garlic, minced

1 Tbsp Italian seasoning

1 tsp kosher salt

1 tsp freshly ground black pepper

3 large carrots, peeled and chopped

3 stalks celery, chopped

2 medium yellow onions, chopped

1 cup bison, beef, or vegetable stock

1 Tbsp unsalted butter

1 Tbsp all-purpose flour

The Big Chief's Wild Rice Pilaf (see opposite page)

Chopped cilantro, for garnish (optional)

Wild rice, which is actually several species of grass, grows wild and has long been an essential ingredient in Aboriginal cuisine. Josh Dockstator serves it with his bison meatballs from his Big Chief food truck in Hamilton. Wild rice is found in most supermarkets, but you can always buy it from canadianwildrice.com.

The Big Chief's Wild Rice Pilaf

Makes 4 servings

In a large saucepan, combine the rice and stock. Bring to a boil over high heat, and then reduce the heat to low and cover. Simmer for 30 minutes. Remove from the heat. Let stand, covered, for 30 minutes. Drain if necessary.

In a large nonstick skillet over medium-high, heat the oil. Add the bell pepper, onion, and garlic. Cook, stirring, until soft, about 8 minutes. Season to taste with salt and pepper. Stir into the wild rice.

1 cup wild rice, rinsed

4 cups bison, beef, or vegetable stock

1 Tbsp extra-virgin olive oil

1 red bell pepper, chopped

½ medium red onion, chopped

2 cloves garlic, minced

Kosher salt

Freshly ground black pepper

"I love how much flavor there is with bison." —Josh Dockstator

One Shot

To be an ethical carnivore, you need to understand how the animals you eat live, and how they die. How our bison live is a lovely story to tell. How they die is a tough one. No matter how humanely it's done, it's not something people want to visualize.

Here's the story of one of our bison, Green Tag 061.

He was born one spring in the Chin Coulee herd and mistakenly labeled a female the following fall in the frenzy of sorting and tagging. Lucky him. He got a green tag, the color the heifers were given that year, instead of the blue tag that the bulls always get. The "061" refers to the year he was born (0 for 2010) plus his assigned number (61).

Instead of staying in the corral to be fed until he reached his slaughter weight, Green Tag 061 was turned back out on the land to munch on shortgrass prairie with the herd.

Rick eventually figured out his mistake, but it took three years for him to get around to moving Green Tag 061 into a corral. Green Tag 061 spent just three months in the corral, eating mostly hay supplemented by vitamin-rich pellets made of lentil and pulse screenings. Then we realized we'd better eat him before his meat got too old and tough.

Wednesday, July 16, 2013: Rick and his one ranch hand, Kevin Street, get up at dawn to coax the skittish bison from the corral, through a passageway called "the chute," and into a trailer attached to our Dodge Ram 3500.

"Easy now, you're all right in there," Kevin says soothingly to the animal, who quiets right down, although he hates being alone. "Easy, kid."

We hit the road at 6:50 A.M. Rick leads in his truck hauling the bison trailer; I trail behind in our van. We drive slowly and carefully down the deserted secondary highways of southern

Alberta. It takes just over an hour to get to Coaldale, home of Prairie Meats, a provincially licensed abattoir and custom butcher.

We park in a gated compound at the side of the building. A provincial inspector—clad in a hard hat, raincoat, and rubber boots—peeks through the trailer window to make sure the bison is alive, standing, and healthy. Prairie Meats owner Andrew Anderson checks that our paperwork is in order, and then gives a third man the okay to point a .22 Magnum into the trailer and fire a single shot into the bison's forehead. Green Tag 061 slumps instantly to the floor with a resounding thump.

"The goal is one shot every time," says Andrew, who shares the responsibility with one other man.

ANDREW ANDERSON

Let's call it 90 minutes from corral to slaughter. That's not a terrible amount of time, although it would be better to use a mobile abattoir so our bison could die at home. Unfortunately, you can't use them in Alberta if you plan to sell your meat.

(One aside here: This was the last "trailer shoot" for our bison. Most animals are unloaded from their trailers and walk inside to a "knock box," but bison are too wild and powerful to use systems built for cows, sheep, and pigs. Prairie Meats is adding extra-high panels so the bison can run inside. It will be in place for our next slaughter.)

The men wrap a chain around the bison's back foot and use a hydraulic lift to haul him out of the trailer and hang him upside down. His throat is slashed so he bleeds out into a bucket before he's moved inside to the "kill floor." His head and feet are removed.

Inside the abattoir, Andrew and I discuss my special requests. I want the organs, and they must be taken and inspected now. We always take the heads to decompose naturally. We let the skulls bleach in the sun. Then we sell them.

The room we're in is stark but not unpleasant. It's mostly concrete floors and metal machinery. There are hoses everywhere so the men can rinse themselves, and the carcass, repeatedly as they work. There's a faint mineral smell in the air, but no stench of blood.

The two men work quickly and quietly. The carcass is lifted with an electric hoist and hung on a hook. Andrew removes the hide with his knife. He tosses organs and intestines into the "gut wagon," a two-level contraption that the inspector uses to examine edible and inedible bits.

Abattoirs are regulated by the meat inspection branch of Alberta Agriculture and Rural Development. Meat inspectors approve healthy animals for slaughter and condemn unhealthy ones. They monitor the slaughter process and examine the carcass, head, internal organs, and lymphatic system.

I stand with the inspector as he pokes and prods our bison bits. Anything that hits the floor while being removed from the carcass is declared contaminated. Nothing does.

I'm curious when a hollow, rippled object that I don't recognize winds up in the gut wagon. It's the trachea, part of the bison's massive windpipe.

"It's clean. It's edible. They'll probably use it for pet food," suggests the inspector. He's right. It will be dehydrated and sold as a protein-rich dog treat.

Andrew, who's wearing waterproof chest waders along with his hard hat, now has the carcass at ground level and is sawing it into two "sides." The compulsive hosing continues. The goal, says Andrew, is to have the carcass "as clean as possible before the stamp goes on and it goes in the cooler." His tool belt is strapped to his waist with a chain.

Green Tag 061 gets his stamp, a declaration that his meat meets food safety standards. His carcass is whisked away. It will be chilled in a blast cooler, and then hung in the holding cooler for 10 to 12 days so the meat firms up and is easier to cut.

Wednesday is "kill day" at Prairie Meats, so the office and retail area are closed. I call in my custom order a few days later to Andrew's wife, Jennifer.

This order is something I always struggle with, and I'm relieved to hear I'm not alone.

"There's a million variations that you can get out of one animal," says Andrew.

The offals are easy. I just circle the ones I want and add in special requests like "cut tail at joints," "package liver in one-pound pieces," and "split femurs lengthwise for marrow."

Sometimes I ask for the meaty soup bones, cut in chunks and bagged with the neck bones, but often I don't.

"You can get overwhelmed with this stuff," agrees Andrew. "You can take too much and it just clogs your freezer."

Rick and I have settled into a routine with steaks and roasts. We like the brisket, tri-tip, flat iron, flank, and skirt left whole. We get striploin (also known as New York strip), tenderloin, top sirloin, and rib-eye steaks cut 1 inch (2.5 centimeters) thick. Cross-ribs and boneless blades are our go-to pot roasts. Short ribs confuse us, and we dabble with three different cuts. The inside and outside round goes to jerky. Eye-of-round roasts are saved for one customer in Medicine Hat.

Then there's "the trim"—the meat that remains after we've taken what we want. This time we want half the trim to be transformed into ground beef, and the other half to be crafted into maple and Italian sausages.

Sure, this all sounds delicious, but then there's all the stuff we're missing. When we take tenderloin and striploin, we miss porterhouse, T-bone, and wing steaks or high-quality kebab meat. We never get "stew meat" (a somewhat random term), choosing instead to slice up our own so we can control where it comes from.

I agonize over these options two weeks later when Andrew lets me return to watch the custom butchering of Green Tag 061. I arrive at 9:00 AM and head to the butchering room, wearing a hairnet and protective clothing as I did at the slaughter. Andrew and another guy are already working hard on my order.

"Right now we're breaking the front quarter," says Andrew, who's wearing a rubber apron and white hard hat. "Right there, Wyatt's got the brisket and front shank for the debone process."

Wyatt Nelson is just 16 years old and a novice, but he's a hunter who learned to butcher deer with his dad and found his calling.

Andrew has owned Prairie Meats since 2007 after working at it for years. "So I never took a formal college meat-cutting course. Everything I learn, I learn on the job."

Prairie Meats does custom butchering of cows, bison, sheep, pigs, lambs, goats, ostriches, emus, and rabbits, as well as wild deer, elk, and moose from hunters.

"Interpreting custom instructions can be hard," grouses Andrew. "A lot of people look at the meat-cut chart and think they're going to get everything on it."

The bison industry doesn't have its own meat-cut chart, so it has adopted the cut names and numbers used for beef, usually from the North American Meat Association (NAMP) or the Institutional Meat Purchase Specifications (IMPS).

Don't let the hair and head fool you—bison aren't as big as they seem. And their meat is extremely lean. Andrew calls it "straight protein."

"If you try to age this for 14 to 28 days like beef, it wouldn't be salvageable because there's no fat cover. It just gets darker and thicker and drier. There's no fat to protect it."

We're finished cutting my steaks and roasts. I've learned a lot that will help me customize future orders, but I am daunted to realize how much there is to know about butchering.

Wyatt is thinly slicing meat for jerky. The trim will be vacuum-sealed and kept in the cooler for a few days until Helena Dyck turns it into sausage, jerky, pepperoni, and burger patties.

Today she's wrapping our meat. For the steaks, roasts, and offals, we prefer butcher's paper to Cryovac. We want ground meat in 1-pound (450-gram) packages, packed in Styrofoam tubs wrapped in butcher's paper. Helena puts a sticker on each package that records the bison's number, the date, and the Prairie Meats plant number.

I usually wait for my meat to be frozen, but all this butchering has made me hungry so I take home a pair of gorgeous rib steaks for a feast. A week later, I return for the rest of my meat. The bill to slaughter and butcher Green Tag 061 comes to $1,071.66.

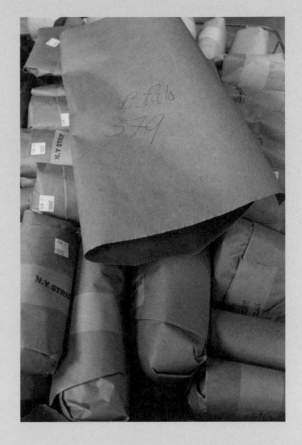

He was a little skinny, about 1,120 pounds (510 kilograms), and his "hot carcass weight" came to 502 pounds (228 kilograms). That's the weight of the unchilled carcass after the hide, head, organs, and intestines are removed. We take home several hundred pounds of meat plus the offals and bags of soup bones.

What a phenomenal amount of great eating for less than five dollars a pound. That's why I urge everyone who wants to eat bison to buy a chest freezer, hook up with a rancher, and custom order a whole animal.

As for Green Tag 061, his age doesn't show and he's absolutely delicious. It was an honor to know him and it is a pleasure to eat him.

CHAPTER 2

Ground
(Beyond Burgers + Balls)

Ground meat is relatively inexpensive, extremely versatile, and easy to cook if you remember (from the last chapter) these three things:

1. Cook until no pink remains.
2. Cook to 160°F if you're using a thermometer (preferably digital).
3. Ground bison doesn't usually shrink and isn't fatty, so you probably won't have to drain the cooked meat.

I get a kick out of making cheesy "buffalo biscuits" using a bison-shaped cookie cutter. My husband would tell you to double the meat. Don't limit yourself to cheddar—lots of cheeses would work well here.

Bison + Cheddar Biscuits

Makes about 12 biscuits

In a medium nonstick skillet over medium-high heat, cook the bison, stirring with a wooden spoon to break up the meat, until it is cooked through, about 6 to 8 minutes. (This should yield about 1 cup.) Let cool.

Preheat the oven to 400°F. Line 1 or 2 baking sheets with parchment paper.

In a medium mixing bowl, stir together the flour, baking powder, and salt. Add the butter. Using your fingers, work the butter into the flour mixture until the mixture resembles coarse crumbs. Add the cheddar and cooked bison. Toss until everything is evenly coated.

Make a well in the center of the mixture. Add the milk. Using a wooden spoon, stir until the mixture comes together as a sticky dough. Transfer the dough to a lightly floured counter and knead by hand about 10 times into a ball.

Using a lightly floured rolling pin, roll out the dough so it is about ½ inch thick. Using a round cookie cutter (about 2 inches in diameter) or a small glass, cut the dough into biscuits. (You can also use cookie cutters in other shapes.) Gather up the pastry scraps and reroll until all of the dough is used.

Place the biscuits on the lined baking sheets. Bake, in batches if needed, until the biscuits are puffed on top and golden on the bottom, about 12 to 15 minutes.

8 oz ground bison

2 cups all-purpose flour

1 Tbsp baking powder

½ tsp kosher salt

¼ cup cold unsalted butter, cut into small pieces

1 cup grated old or extra-old cheddar

1 cup milk

Here's my spin on Latin American empanadas but made with frozen puff pastry instead of homemade dough. These savory turnovers are a meal in themselves when served with a salad on the side. They taste even better with Chimichurri Sauce (p. 86).

Bison Puffs

Makes 8 puffs

Defrost the pastry as per the package instructions, either overnight in the fridge or on the counter for 2 hours. Separate into 2 blocks.

On a lightly floured surface using a floured rolling pin, roll out each block into a 12-inch square. Cut each square in 4. You will have 8 pieces.

Preheat the oven to 400°F. Line 2 baking sheets with parchment paper.

In a large nonstick skillet over medium-high, heat the oil. Add the onion, carrot, celery, and garlic. Cook, stirring, for 8 minutes to soften. Add the bison. Cook, stirring and breaking up the meat with a wooden spoon, until it is just cooked through. Remove from the heat. Stir in the olives and egg. Season to taste with salt and pepper.

Divide the bison mixture evenly over the puff pastry pieces (about ¼ cup for each). Moisten the pastry edges with water. Fold the dough over the filling to make triangles. Press firmly and pinch to seal the edges.

Place the puffs on the prepared baking sheets. Bake until the pastries are browned and puffed, about 15 to 20 minutes.

1 (14 oz) package frozen puff pastry

1 Tbsp extra-virgin olive oil

½ medium yellow onion, finely chopped

½ large carrot, peeled and finely chopped

½ stalk celery, finely chopped

1 clove garlic, minced

8 oz ground bison

¼ cup chopped pitted black or green olives

1 hard-boiled egg, peeled and diced

Kosher salt

Freshly ground black pepper

Diva Q is a competitive barbecue and *BBQ Crawl* television celebrity who doubles as Barrie mom Danielle Dimovski. She's an extreme extrovert with a big personality, so it's no surprise that she puts the whole batch of this assertive taco seasoning in with her ground meat. Find out more about Danielle at divaq.ca.

Diva Q's Bold Bison Taco Salad

Makes 4 servings

For the taco seasoning, in a small bowl, combine the chili powder, paprika, cumin, salt, pepper, chipotle powder, garlic powder, onion powder, and red pepper flakes.

For the salad, in a medium skillet over medium, heat the oil. Add the onion. Cook, stirring, for 7 minutes. Raise the heat to medium-high. Add the bison and taco seasoning. Cook, stirring, for 5 minutes. Add the water. Stir thoroughly. Simmer for 5 to 10 minutes, until the bison is cooked through.

To serve, place a layer of lettuce on each plate or in each bowl. Top each with the spiced bison. Crumble the tortilla chips over the meat. Top with the cheese, tomatoes, avocado, salsa, sour cream, black beans, and cilantro. (If you prefer, you can serve everything in separate serving bowls so people can personalize their salads.)

TACO SEASONING:

1½ Tbsp pure mild chili powder (such as ancho)

1½ Tbsp smoked paprika

1 tsp ground cumin

1 tsp kosher salt

1 tsp freshly ground black pepper

½ tsp chipotle powder

½ tsp garlic powder

½ tsp onion powder

½ tsp red pepper flakes

SALAD:

2 Tbsp canola oil

1 medium red onion, finely chopped

1 lb ground bison

½ cup water

1 head iceberg lettuce, chopped

1 large bag tortilla chips (preferably multicolored) (about 4 cups)

2 cups grated old cheddar

1 cup chopped tomatoes

1 avocado, pitted, peeled, and sliced

½ cup prepared salsa

½ cup sour cream

½ cup canned black beans, drained and rinsed

¼ cup chopped cilantro

When my daughter Lucy was in Grade 6 and living at our ranch for a year, she played basketball and volleyball at Foremost School. The most popular item at the canteen was taco in a bag. Picture an opened bag of Doritos (cheese nachos) topped with taco fixings and served with a fork sticking out of it. Lucy is a vegetarian so she didn't try it, but I couldn't resist. It turns out that this portable meal is wildly popular at schools and fairs across North America, and it's fun to serve at home if you're having a movie night or backyard picnic. For DIY taco seasoning, use Diva Q's blend (see p. 55) or make your own, using a mix of pure chili powder, paprika, cumin, garlic powder, onion powder, red chili flakes, oregano, salt, and pepper.

Bison Tacos in a Bag

Makes 4 servings

In a large nonstick skillet over medium-high, heat the oil. Add the bison. Cook, stirring, until the meat is browned and cooked through, about 6 to 8 minutes. Add the seasoning. Cook, stirring, for 2 minutes. Transfer the meat to a bowl.

Leaving the bags of tortilla chips unopened and gently crush the chips by hand. Then, using scissors, snip open the bags along the long (side) edge. Spoon equal portions of bison mixture into each bag. Serve the toppings separately, so people can add their own lettuce, tomatoes, cheese, salsa, and sour cream.

1 Tbsp canola oil

1 lb ground bison

¼ cup Tex-Mex spice blend or homemade taco seasoning, or 1 (1¼ oz) packet taco seasoning

4 individual-size bags of nacho cheese–flavored tortilla chips (such as Doritos), unopened

OPTIONAL TOPPINGS:
Shredded iceberg lettuce
Diced tomatoes
Grated cheddar
Prepared salsa
Sour cream

I found this idea while trolling the Internet for Super Bowl meal ideas for work. I don't like the taste of those taco seasoning packets, so I make my own using whatever mix of pure chili powder, herbs, and spices I'm in the mood for. I've listed a bunch in the headnote on the previous page; sometimes I'll use coriander and cayenne too. If you're not feeding a crowd, cut this recipe in half.

Bison Taco Ring

Makes 16 pieces (for 8 main or 16 appetizer servings)

Heat a large skillet over medium-high. Add the bison. Cook, stirring and breaking up the meat with a wooden spoon, until it's no longer pink, about 6 minutes. Add the seasoning and water. Bring to a boil, and then reduce the heat to medium and cook, stirring often, until the liquid is absorbed, about 6 minutes. Remove from the heat and stir in the cheese until melted.

Preheat the oven to 375°F. Grease a large round pizza tray or baking pan or a pizza stone.

Unroll the dough from the tubes. Working along the perforations, separate each tube of dough into 8 triangles. Arrange the triangles on the tray with the short bottom edges facing in, going around the tray so that you end up with a large circular opening in the center of the tray. The triangles should overlap slightly, and the top of each dough triangle will probably hang over the edge of the pan. Spread the bison mixture along the inside edge of the circle. Fold the top pointy end of each triangle over the filling, tucking the point under the inside edge. The filling won't be completely covered.

Bake until the pastry is puffed and golden, about 10 to 13 minutes.

To serve, fill the center of your taco ring with whatever combination of cheese, lettuce, onion, tomato, and olives you like. Serve bowls of salsa and sour cream separately.

1 lb ground bison

3 Tbsp homemade taco seasoning or Tex-Mex spice blend

1 cup water

1 cup grated old cheddar

2 tubes refrigerated crescent rolls (each with 8 rolls)

OPTIONAL ACCOMPANIMENTS:
Grated cheddar

Shredded iceberg lettuce

Chopped yellow onions

Diced tomatoes

Chopped pitted black olives

Prepared salsa

Sour cream

Quinoa and kale are two supernutritious foods that have enjoyed a few years in the culinary spotlight. I combine them whenever possible, and tossing them into a soup with ground bison just makes sense.

Quinoa + Kale Bison Soup

Makes about 10 cups (for 6 large servings)

In a large saucepan over medium, heat the oil. Add the onion, bell pepper, jalapeno, and garlic. Cook, stirring, for 5 minutes to soften. Add the bison. Cook, stirring, for another 5 minutes to brown and partially cook the meat. Add the stock or water. Raise the heat to high and bring to a boil. Add the quinoa. Reduce the heat to low and cover. Simmer for 13 minutes. Stir in the kale until it wilts. Simmer for 5 minutes. Season to taste with the Sriracha, salt, and pepper.

1 Tbsp extra-virgin olive oil

1 medium yellow onion, chopped

1 red bell pepper, chopped

1 jalapeno, minced with seeds

4 large cloves garlic, minced

1 lb ground bison

8 cups bison or vegetable stock and/or water

1 cup white, red, and/or black quinoa, rinsed

4 cups trimmed and chopped kale leaves

Sriracha (Asian hot sauce), to taste

Kosher salt

Freshly ground black pepper

In Grande Prairie, Alberta, local food advocate Matthew Toni is the executive chef of Maddhatters (maddhatters.com). He relies on Glendean Farms (glendeanfarms.com) for his bison. He buys the whole animal, gives his chefs a weekly "butcher's cut feature," and does a lot of grinding and braising. As for this meatloaf, Matthew says, "I just wanted to create a meatloaf that everybody can relate to but that's jazzed up a little bit." Since so many people grew up on burnt meatloaf, the chef plays with that memory by searing his.

Glendean Farms Bison Meatloaf

Makes 6 servings

In a food processor, purée the onion and garlic.

In a large bowl, whisk 1½ tablespoons of the ketchup with the mustard, Worcestershire sauce, and hot sauce.

In a small bowl, stir together the panko, oregano, pepper, and salt. Add to the ketchup mixture, along with the onion mixture and the bison. Mix well by hand.

Place parchment paper in a 9 × 5 × 3-inch loaf pan, with parchment hanging over the sides. Add the meatloaf, packing it in firmly and smoothing the top.

Cover the meatloaf with the overhanging parchment paper. Place an empty loaf pan on top of the parchment. Fill with soup cans or weights. Refrigerate overnight to help meatloaf firm up before frying. When ready, remove the meatloaf from the loaf pan and pat it dry with paper towels. Season to taste with pepper.

Preheat the oven to 375°F.

In a large nonstick skillet over medium-high, heat the oil. Sear the top and bottom of the meatloaf for 2 minutes each, until both sides are brown. Use two large metal spatulas to flip it.

Line the loaf pan with fresh parchment paper. Return the meatloaf to the pan. Brush the top with the remaining 1½ tablespoons of ketchup. Insert an ovenproof digital thermometer.

Bake until the thermometer registers 160°F, about 40 minutes. Drain any juices. Let cool for 10 minutes before slicing.

Eat leftover meatloaf cold, or heat a little oil in a medium skillet over medium-high and sear slices until browned and hot.

½ medium yellow onion, chopped

2 cloves garlic, minced

3 Tbsp ketchup, divided

1½ Tbsp Dijon mustard

2½ tsp Worcestershire sauce

1 tsp hot sauce

½ cup panko (Japanese bread crumbs)

2 tsp dried oregano leaves

1 tsp freshly ground black pepper

½ tsp kosher salt

1½ lb ground bison

2 tsp canola oil

People are usually surprised to discover that American media mogul Ted Turner is also a bison rancher who co-owns a chain of restaurants called Ted's Montana Grill (tedsmontanagrill.com). Bison plays a key role on the menu. This chili, created by Ted's personal chef, Karen Averitt, is one of the restaurant's signature dishes. Pinto beans are a welcome change from red kidney beans. Flying D, by the way, is one of Ted's ranches in Montana.

Karen's "Flying D" Bison Chili

Makes 2 servings

In a large pot over medium-high heat, cook the bison, stirring with a wooden spoon to break up large pieces, for 5 minutes. Add the yellow onion and garlic. Cook, stirring, until soft, about 5 to 7 minutes.

In a measuring cup, combine the warm water, tomato paste, and beef bouillon concentrate. Whisk well. Add to the pot. Bring to a boil. Add the oregano, chili powder, cumin, sugar, cayenne pepper, and black pepper. Reduce the heat to medium-low. Simmer for 15 minutes. Add the beans and tomatoes. Simmer for 1 minute.

Serve chili topped, if desired, with cheese, red onions, and jalapenos.

1 lb ground bison

½ cup diced yellow onion

2 tsp minced garlic

1½ cups warm water

6 Tbsp tomato paste

1 Tbsp liquid beef bouillon concentrate

½ tsp dried oregano leaves

4 tsp chili powder

1¼ tsp ground cumin

1 tsp granulated sugar

Pinch cayenne pepper

Pinch freshly ground black pepper

½ cup canned pinto beans, drained and rinsed

½ cup fresh diced tomatoes or canned diced tomatoes with liquid

OPTIONAL TOPPINGS:
Grated cheddar

Finely diced red onions

Chopped jalapenos

Head-Smashed-In Buffalo Jump is a World Heritage site with an interpretive center near Fort Macleod in southern Alberta. Inside, the Buffalo Jump Café is run by Bryan McEvoy, general manager of Mac's Catering. His cook, Ania Marzec, shared this recipe with me. This is a beautiful, old-school chili recipe that's tame enough for kids but can be spiced up at the end. For more on the jump, check out headsmashedin.org.

Head-Smashed-In Buffalo Jump's Bison Chili

Makes about 8 cups (for 4 large or 8 small servings)

Heat a large saucepan over medium-high. Add the bison. Cook, stirring and breaking up the meat with a wooden spoon, for 5 minutes. Sprinkle with the chili powder and garlic powder. Cook, stirring, for 2 minutes. Transfer the meat to a bowl.

Add the oil and butter to the saucepan. When the butter melts, add the bell pepper, onion, and mushrooms. Cook, stirring, for 5 minutes. Return the bison mixture to the saucepan. Add the beans, pasta sauce, and water. Bring to a boil over high heat, and then reduce the heat to low and simmer for 45 minutes, adding water if needed to reach desired consistency. Season to taste with salt, black pepper, and cayenne pepper.

Serve the chili with bannock, if desired.

1 lb ground bison

1 Tbsp chili powder

2 tsp garlic powder

1 Tbsp canola oil

1 Tbsp unsalted butter

1 green bell pepper, diced

1 medium yellow onion, diced

8 oz white button or cremini mushrooms, sliced

1 (19 oz) can red kidney beans, drained and rinsed

3 cups tomato-basil pasta sauce

1 cup water

Kosher salt

Freshly ground black pepper

Cayenne pepper

Head-Smashed-In Buffalo Jump's Baked Bannock (optional, see opposite page)

Bannock is Aboriginal soul food. It's a bread that can be deep-fried, baked in an oven, or baked over an open fire. It's a deceptively simple recipe that is harder to perfect than you'd imagine. Just be gentle. Ania Marzec from the Buffalo Jump Café at Head-Smashed-In Buffalo Jump shared this version.

Head-Smashed-In Buffalo Jump's Baked Bannock

Makes 8 servings

Preheat the oven to 400°F. Grease a rimmed baking sheet.

In a medium mixing bowl, whisk together the flour, baking powder, and salt. Add 1 cup of the water. Mix gently, first with a fork and then by hand, until the mixture just comes together as dough, adding the remaining ¼ cup of water by the tablespoon as needed.

Transfer to a lightly floured counter and knead gently 10 times. Do not overmix or the bannock will be tough. Pat into a flat disk that's about 1 inch thick and about 8 to 9 inches in diameter.

Transfer to the baking sheet. Bake until the top of the bread is golden, about 15 to 25 minutes. Serve warm. For leftovers, wrap well in plastic and eat within 2 days, reheating in the microwave if desired.

3 cups presifted unbleached all-purpose flour
1½ tsp baking powder
½ tsp table or fine sea salt
1¼ cups water, divided

Linda Hubalek (lindasbuffalomeatrecipes.com) won the 2001 best chili award at the National Bison Association's annual conference with this recipe. It was served at the banquet. Linda and her husband have retired from the bison business but still have a small herd in Kansas. She writes about Kansas pioneer women and promotes bison at bisonfarm.com. White chili usually has white beans, white meat, and no tomatoes, so this is technically an "almost white chili."

Smoky Hill Bison White Chili

Makes 4 servings

In a medium saucepan over medium-high heat, cook the bison, using a wooden spoon to break up the meat, until browned, about 7 minutes. Add the oil, onion, celery, garlic, and chilies. Cook, stirring, for 5 to 7 minutes to soften.

Meanwhile, in a blender, combine half of the beans with the flour and milk. Purée. Add to the bison mixture along with the remaining beans, water, vinegar, lime juice, chili powder, salt, pepper, and cumin. Bring just to a simmer, and then reduce the heat to low. Simmer, stirring often, for 30 minutes. Stir in the Sriracha, if desired.

Serve bowls of chili topped with mozzarella, sour cream, cilantro, and paprika, if desired.

1 lb ground bison
2 Tbsp extra-virgin olive oil
1 small yellow onion, chopped
1 stalk celery, chopped
1 clove garlic, minced
½ (4 oz) can diced green chilies (about ¼ cup)
1 (19 oz) can white beans (such as kidney/ cannellini, navy, great northern, or butter), drained and rinsed
3 Tbsp all-purpose flour
1 cup milk
1 cup water
1 Tbsp white vinegar
Juice of 1 lime
1 Tbsp chili powder
½ tsp kosher salt
¼ tsp freshly ground black pepper
¼ tsp ground cumin
2 to 3 tsp Sriracha or other hot sauce, to taste (optional)

OPTIONAL TOPPINGS:
Grated mozzarella
Sour cream
Chopped cilantro
Paprika

During a trip to Great Falls, Montana, my husband, Rick, discovered a "wheat chili mix" at the Wheat Montana bakery (wheatmontana.com). Along with a seasoning packet, it was filled with hard wheat berries—something Rick grows. As the bakery crowed, "it's a real Prairie taste." Wheat berries (whole unprocessed kernels) are sold at health and bulk food stores and some supermarkets, and can be hard or soft. This is my version of that chili.

Bison Wheat Berry Chili

Makes 4 to 6 servings

In a medium saucepan, combine the wheat berries and water. Bring to a boil over high heat. Reduce the heat to medium-low and simmer, covered, until chewy-tender, about 30 to 45 minutes, depending on the age of the berries. Add more water if needed while cooking. Drain.

In a large saucepan over medium, heat the oil. Add the onion. Cook, stirring, for 6 minutes to soften. Add the garlic and bison. Cook, breaking up the meat with a wooden spoon, for 7 minutes. Stir in the chili powder, oregano, and cumin. Cook, stirring, for 1 minute. Add the cooked wheat berries, tomatoes with their juices, and stock or water. Raise the heat to high and bring to a boil, and then reduce the heat to low and simmer, covered, for 1 hour. Stir in the corn. Season to taste with salt and pepper. Simmer for 10 minutes.

1 cup dried wheat berries (hard wheat kernels), rinsed

3 cups water

2 Tbsp canola oil

1 medium yellow onion, diced

4 large cloves garlic, minced

1 lb ground bison

1 tsp pure chili powder

1 tsp dried oregano leaves

1 tsp ground cumin

1 (28 oz) can diced tomatoes

1½ cups bison or beef stock or water

1 cup fresh or frozen corn

Kosher salt

Freshly ground black pepper

In my Westernized take on dan dan noodles (a famous Sichuan dish), bison stands in for pork or beef, and I use fresh bean sprouts instead of preserved vegetables. Sichuan peppercorns (sometimes labeled prickly ash) have a lemony kick and will make your tongue tingle. Chinese sesame sauce is a thick paste similar to tahini except that the sesames are roasted. Chili oil is usually sesame and corn oil blended with chili peppers. Pick a noodle thickness that appeals to you. I prefer thicker noodles.

Spicy Sichuan Noodles with Bison

Makes 2 servings

In a small bowl, soak the chilies in hot water for 15 minutes, until pliable. Slice each in half and remove the seeds.

In a wok or large nonstick skillet over medium-high, heat the peanut oil. Add the chilies and peppercorns. Cook, stirring, for 30 seconds, until the oil is fragrant. Do not burn the spices. Add the bean sprouts. Cook, stirring, for 1 minute. Add the bison and soy sauce. Cook, stirring and breaking up the meat with a wooden spoon, until the meat is cooked through, browned and crisp, about 6 to 8 minutes. Remove the chilies if possible (don't eat them).

Meanwhile, bring a large saucepan of water to a boil over high heat. Add the noodles and cook according to the package instructions. Drain. Transfer to a mixing bowl.

For the sauce, in a small bowl, whisk together Sichuan pepper, sesame sauce or tahini, soy sauce, and chili oil. Add to the noodles in the mixing bowl. Toss well. Add the meat mixture; toss well.

Cooking Tip: For DIY chili oil, place 2 tablespoons of red chili flakes in a glass jar with a lid. In a small saucepan over medium-high, heat ½ cup of peanut or canola oil until just smoking, about 5 minutes. Remove from the heat and wait for 2 minutes, and then pour the oil over the chili flakes in the jar. Let this mixture cool to room temperature before screwing on the lid. The oil can be stored at room temperature for several months. Use strained or unstrained.

5 small dried red chilies

1 Tbsp peanut oil

1 tsp whole Sichuan peppercorns

½ cup bean sprouts, washed and dried

8 oz ground bison

2 Tbsp soy sauce

8 oz fresh Chinese flour noodles

SAUCE:

½ tsp whole Sichuan peppercorns, toasted and ground

2 Tbsp Chinese sesame sauce or tahini

¼ cup soy sauce

¼ cup Asian chili oil (see Cooking Tip)

This is my take on the spicy Sichuan dish called mapo tofu. Bison stands in for ground pork or beef. I like my tofu crumbled, but it's more traditional for it to be cubed. Chili bean sauce (toban djan or douban jiang) is a paste made from salted chili pepper and fermented soybean. Visit an Asian supermarket for the toban djan and black beans. Sichuan peppercorns are tiny, dark red-brown berries from a shrub that crack open white and have some tiny stems.

Spicy Sichuan Bison + Tofu Stir-Fry

Makes 2 to 3 servings

In a large nonstick skillet or wok over medium-high, heat the oil. Add the bison. Cook, stirring with a wooden spoon to break up the meat, until it is cooked through, about 7 minutes. Add the chili bean sauce, black beans, and cayenne pepper or chili powder. Stir-fry for 1 minute. Add 1 cup of the water and the soy sauce, sugar, and tofu. Reduce the heat to medium and simmer for 5 minutes.

In a small bowl, whisk together the cornstarch and remaining 1 tablespoon of water until the cornstarch is dissolved. Stir into the bison mixture to thicken. Simmer, stirring, for 1 minute. Add the green onions. Simmer for 1 minute to soften them. Stir in the Sichuan pepper.

1 Tbsp peanut or canola oil

8 oz ground bison

3 Tbsp chili bean sauce (toban djan)

1 Tbsp fermented black beans, rinsed and drained (or substitute dried salted black beans)

2 tsp cayenne pepper or pure chili powder

1 cup plus 1 Tbsp water, divided

1 Tbsp soy sauce

1 tsp granulated sugar

1 lb medium tofu, patted dry and crumbled

1 Tbsp cornstarch

5 green onions, thinly sliced

½ tsp whole Sichuan peppercorns, toasted and ground

Meat-stuffed peppers are a blank slate awaiting your creative touch. I've made these ones simply with cumin and paprika, but any dried spices or fresh herbs would work. I like bulgur for its taste, couscous because it's ready in a snap, and rice when I'm feeling traditional.

Multicolored Bell Peppers Stuffed with Bison

Makes 6 peppers

Preheat the oven to 350°F.

Slice ½ inch off the top of each pepper. Discard the top of the stems, the seeds, and the white membranes. Reserve the tops.

In a large skillet over medium, heat the oil. Add the onion and garlic. Cook, stirring, for 7 minutes to soften. Add the bison. Cook, breaking up the meat with a wooden spoon, just until the meat is no longer pink, about 6 minutes. Stir in the cumin and paprika. Season to taste with salt and pepper. Stir in the bulgur, couscous, or brown rice.

Stuff the peppers with equal portions of the bison mixture, packing loosely or tightly as needed. Pack the peppers upright in a single layer in a large ovenproof saucepan or deep casserole dish. Place the top back on each pepper. Pour the tomato sauce all around the peppers. Cover and bake for 60 to 90 minutes, checking after 60 minutes, until the peppers are desired tenderness.

Serve the peppers topped with the sauce they were cooked in.

6 large red, orange, or yellow bell peppers

1 Tbsp canola oil

1 medium yellow onion, finely diced

3 large cloves garlic, minced

1 lb ground bison

1 tsp ground cumin

1 tsp paprika

Kosher salt

Freshly ground black pepper

2 cups cooked medium bulgur (see Cooking Tip), couscous, or brown rice

3 cups tomato sauce

Cooking Tip: Bulgur is parboiled, dried, and cracked wheat. It comes in fine, medium, and coarse grinds. Put 1 cup medium bulgur in a bowl. Pour 2 cups of boiling water over it and cover. Let stand for 20 minutes, until the bulgur is rehydrated and plumped. Fluff it with a fork. You should have about 2 cups.

I love the idea of cabbage rolls, but not the usually bland taste or the fussiness of making the rolls. Here I've jacked up the flavor with lots of smoked paprika and parsley, and added texture with chickpeas. I also urge you to try tender, sweet Savoy cabbage instead of the more traditional green cabbage.

Smoky Bison Cabbage Roll Casserole

Makes 8 servings

Place the shredded cabbage in a large bowl or pot. Cover with boiling water. Let stand for 15 minutes to soften. Drain well.

Meanwhile, in a large nonstick skillet over medium, heat the oil. Add the onion and garlic. Cook, stirring, for 6 minutes to soften. Add the bison and raise the heat to medium-high. Cook, stirring and breaking up the meat with a wooden spoon, until cooked through, about 7 minutes. Stir in the paprika. Cook, stirring, for 1 minute. Transfer to a large bowl. Stir in the chickpeas, rice, and parsley. Season to taste with salt and pepper. Stir in 2 cups of the tomato sauce.

Preheat the oven to 375°F.

Spread ½ cup of the tomato sauce over the bottom of a 13 × 9-inch or large round 12-cup baking dish. Cover the bottom with a layer of cabbage. Top with about 2 cups of the bison mixture. Continue layering until all the ingredients are used, ending with cabbage. Pour the remaining 1½ cups of tomato sauce over everything. Cover with foil.

Bake until the cabbage is tender and the sauce is bubbling, about 1 hour. Remove the foil. Let stand for 10 minutes before serving.

1 small Savoy cabbage, cored and shredded

1 Tbsp canola oil

1 large yellow onion, chopped

5 large cloves garlic, minced

1 lb ground bison

2 Tbsp smoked paprika

1 (19 oz) can chickpeas, drained and rinsed

2 cups cooked brown rice

½ cup chopped flat-leaf parsley

Kosher salt

Freshly ground black pepper

4 cups tomato sauce, divided

Canadian food enthusiast Anita Stewart turned me on to this savory pie with impeccable local pedigree. She got the recipe from Debbie Demers of Earlton, Ontario, who uses local bison, preserved garlic scapes from Quebec, and cheddar from Thornloe Cheese (thornloecheese.ca). Debbie works at Earlton RV and her boss is bison rancher Pierre Belanger. Pierre's Bisons du Nord ranch on the Trans-Canada Highway is home to Canada's largest bison sculpture. Made of steel and fiberglass, it is 19 feet (6 meters) high, 27 feet (8 meters) long, and weighs about 9 tons (8,000 kilograms).

Northern Ontario Bison + Cheddar Pie

Makes 6 servings

In a large heavy skillet over medium-high heat, brown the bison for 7 minutes, using a wooden spoon to break up the meat. Add the onion, celery, and garlic or garlic scapes. Cook, stirring, until the vegetables are tender, about 5 minutes. Stir in the pepper, chili powder, hot sauce, and Worcestershire sauce. Cook, stirring, for 1 minute.

In a small bowl, whisk together the stock and cornstarch. Stir into the bison mixture. Add the cheddar. Stir until cheese melts. Taste; season with salt if desired. Let the mixture cool for 10 minutes.

Preheat the oven to 350°F.

Line the bottom of a 10-inch deep-dish pie plate with 1 of the pie crusts, crimping the edges. Pour the bison-cheese mixture evenly into the unbaked shell. Top with the remaining pie crust. Crimp the edges. Cut several small slits in the top crust.

Bake until the top is golden brown, about 40 to 45 minutes. Let the pie stand for about 15 minutes before serving with black-currant syrup, if desired.

1½ lb ground bison

1 medium yellow onion, chopped

1 stalk celery with leaves, chopped

1 Tbsp minced garlic, or 2 Tbsp minced garlic scapes (fresh or preserved in oil)

1 tsp freshly ground black pepper

1 tsp chili powder

1 tsp hot sauce

1 tsp Worcestershire sauce

1 cup bison or beef stock

2 Tbsp cornstarch

1½ cups grated old cheddar

Kosher salt

2 (10-inch) deep-dish pie crusts

Blackcurrant syrup, for serving (optional)

" I use bison in almost any recipe that calls for ground beef or ground turkey. The taste is great in that it does not have a wild game flavor. I have yet to have someone turn away a plate when I am serving bison meatballs or any other recipe I might adventure into."
—Debbie Demers

Sharlyn Carter-Smith (marketgypsy.ca) lives in Red Deer with her husband, Ivan Smith. They run Big Bend Bison Ranches and Big Bend Market. Sharlyn, who is from the Northwest Territories, shared these perogies, which make her think of "home, my grandmother who has passed away, and our story of how it has all come together. It combines all that I love: my Ukrainian heritage and Ivan's bison." It's almost impossible to get the wrapper/filling ratio exact, so be creative: cook up any extra filling and eat it with rice, or fill any remaining wrappers with something else. Herbes de Provence is a dried spice blend that usually includes rosemary, marjoram, thyme, and summer savory.

Big Bend Bison Perogies

Makes about 24 to 28 perogies (for 4 to 6 servings)

For the dough, put the egg in a 2-cup measure. Whisk until foamy. Add the oil. Bring warm water up to the 1-cup mark on the measuring cup. Whisk well.

In a large bowl, whisk together the flour and salt. Gradually stir in the egg mixture. Stir and knead until it feels like bread dough and is elastic and shiny. Turn the dough out onto a lightly floured counter. Place a bowl overtop. Let the dough rest for 30 minutes.

Meanwhile, for the filling, in a medium mixing bowl, combine the bison, onion, herbes de Provence, and salt. Mix well by hand. Refrigerate until ready to use.

On a lightly floured counter, roll out the dough as thinly as possible, about ¼ inch thick or at least 16 inches in diameter. Using a cookie cutter or drinking glass, cut into 3-inch circles, rerolling scraps. You should have 24 to 28 circles. Cover the dough circles with a clean, damp kitchen towel as you work, to keep them from drying out.

To stuff the perogies, put 1 teaspoon of the raw filling in the center of each dough circle. Fold the dough in half and pinch/seal each side together to create half moons. Make sure there are no cracks or the filling will spill out. If desired, bring the two opposite ends together and join them, making a circle (so that the melted butter will nestle in the cooked perogies). You may have some filling or dough circles left over, so find another use for them.

DOUGH:
1 large egg
2 Tbsp extra-virgin olive oil
Warm water
2½ cups all-purpose flour
1 tsp kosher salt

FILLING:
8 oz ground bison
½ medium yellow onion, finely chopped
½ tsp herbes de Provence
¼ tsp kosher salt

PEROGIES:
6 cups bison or beef stock
Melted butter (optional)
Chopped fresh dill (optional)
Sour cream (optional)

Cook immediately or refrigerate, covered, for several hours until ready to cook. If freezing, place the perogies on a floured baking sheet and place the sheet in the freezer. Once frozen, transfer the perogies to an airtight freezer bag. (Increase the boiling time by a few minutes if cooking from frozen.)

To cook the perogies, in a medium saucepan over high heat, bring the stock to a boil. Add 6 perogies at a time. When the stock returns to a boil, reduce the heat to medium-high. Watch, stirring gently, until the perogies float to the top, and then cook for 1 more minute (it should be about 6 minutes total). Remove the cooked perogies with a slotted spoon and repeat with remaining perogies.

To serve, ladle a little cooking broth into each bowl. Add the perogies. Top with your desired combination of butter, dill, and sour cream.

These fun lollipops from personal gourmet chef and caterer Mark Wrigley and Andrea Bieman, both of Clayoquot Cuisine, are great at cocktail parties. "Everybody seems to love everything on sticks," says Mark, who's the son of Dr. Bob Wrigley, the retired curator of the Assiniboine Park Zoo in Winnipeg. (Read about the senior Wrigley's connection to white bison on page 155.)

Bison Lollipops

Makes 24 lollipops

In a bowl, combine the bison, onion, garlic, rosemary, barbecue sauce, and mustard. Season to taste with salt and pepper. Divide the mixture into 24 balls (each about 1 ounce) by the heaping tablespoonful. Refrigerate, covered, for at least 1 hour to firm up.

Preheat the oven to 375°F.

Pat each ball into a disk that's about 1 inch thick and 1½ inches wide. Wrap the bacon strips around the edges of the bison disks, making sure the ends of the bacon overlap. Stick the skewers through the bison lollipops, starting at the bacon seam.

Place the skewers on a baking sheet. Bake until the bacon is crisp and the meat is cooked through, about 15 to 25 minutes.

Arrange the skewers on a platter. If desired, dollop a little barbecue sauce on the center of the bison portion of each lollipop. Let them cool for 10 minutes before serving.

1 lb ground bison

½ medium white onion, finely diced

3 cloves garlic, minced

1 tsp finely chopped fresh rosemary

1 Tbsp barbecue sauce (preferably Bull's-Eye Bold Original) + more for garnish

1 Tbsp Dijon mustard

Kosher salt

Cracked or freshly ground black pepper

12 strips bacon, halved crosswise

24 short (about 6 inches) wooden skewers, soaked for at least 1 hour in water

"Bison has got some incredible flavors and textures. It's nice to use it as an alternative. It's a healthier choice." —Mark Wrigley

The Dinner Plates of Paris

Most of our animals disappear into a bison-shaped black hole. Rick calls "Anne from Bouvry," and, before you know it, the buffs are loaded on a truck and whisked away.

Young heifers, older cows, yearling bulls, bulls at slaughter weight, this mysterious Anne seems happy to buy them all. But all I know about Bouvry Exports is that it's a French company with Canadian offices, and it ships most of our bison meat to Europe. Or, as Rick romantically spins it, "Our buffalo winds up on the dinner plates of Paris."

Still, this bison black hole haunts me, and, to be honest, I hate that most of our meat leaves Canada. Finally, one day, I decide to end the mystery. I simply call Anne and invite myself over so I can find out where our bison go and how they're treated.

It's a two-hour drive from the ranch to Bouvry's federal slaughterhouse in Fort Macleod. Anne Garrido is the bison manager. She grew up on a farm in France with three cows and a horse, studied agribusiness management, and worked in France, Quebec, and South America before landing in Alberta.

Clad in jeans, a gray sweatshirt, and black work boots, with sunglasses perched on top of her head, she's restless and clearly happiest outside, not at a desk. It's also immediately obvious that Anne loves the challenge and excitement of bison.

I'm momentarily excited to learn that Bouvry ships bison meat to Quebec. "Your bison usually grade well, so they go to Europe," Anne quickly clarifies. "Anything that gets an A1, A2, or A3 grade goes to Europe. That's usually from a healthy, young bull that's not too fat."

She shows me the Canadian bison grading chart, with age categories for youthful

ANNE GARRIDO AND GADJO

and mature, and quality categories to rate muscling, fat color, meat color, and fat measure. Bison that are graded A4, B1, B2, or B3 generally stay in North America.

There's nothing wrong any of these meats. A4 meat, Anne explains, might just be
from a heifer that is a teensy bit too fat. "Heifers are programmed to be mothers, so
they age really fast. If you push them too hard, they get fat. If you don't push them, they
get old."

We chat in an empty, sterile office. There are no bison being slaughtered (that happens Thursdays) or butchered (that happens Monday mornings).

Anne comes to the plant once or twice each week but lives at Bouvry's farm/feedlot
just west of Calgary.

"Feedlot" is my least favorite ranching word, but now seems like a good time to
address it. After various types of animals reach a certain weight from grazing, they may

be transferred to pens to be fattened for slaughter. Multistage beef cattle feedlots can hold thousands of animals eating a diet that's mainly grain. These animals often get growth hormones and antibiotics mixed with their feed and water.

At our ranch, we have two corrals near the house. Each can hold up to 20 bison for about a year, starting when they're weaned at 7 months old. The corrals are almost always reserved for bulls. Rick feeds them a diet that's about 95 percent hay (usually our own, but sometimes supplemented by other farmers' hay when we have a small crop) and 5 percent lentil-based pellets. These Bull's Eye D backgrounding pellets are made by Landmark Feeds in Medicine Hat. They're 88 percent lentil and pulse screenings, 5 percent oat hulls, and 5 percent mixed barley/wheat. The remaining 2 percent includes limestone, salt, vegetable fat, and calcium phosphate, magnesium oxide, and other vitamins and minerals.

Technically, I suppose, we have a small, farm-based feedlot, but it's not a word we use. We don't use growth hormones (nobody does with bison) and never use antibiotics or even deworming treatments. Meanwhile, our bison cows, heifers, late calves, and breeding bulls live year-round on the open range, rotating through various pastures so they don't overgraze an area. They live and die out there. We don't help them with childbirth.

Bouvry demands naturally raised bison that have never been treated with antibiotics, growth hormones, or various other substances. Anne does give each bison one preventive shot of antibiotics when it arrives, but doesn't add it to their feed.

She oversees anywhere from 1,000 animals in the summer to 3,000 over the winter. They eat mostly grass or hay and a 20 percent ration of whole oats. They are split up by gender and age, and may spend time in both the fields and the corrals.

Here are some numbers to ponder: Bouvry slaughters heifers when they reach about 900 pounds (410 kilograms), usually between 24 and 28 months of age. It slaughters bulls at 1,200 pounds (540 kilograms), usually around 30 months. Most animals yield 550 pounds (250 kilograms) of meat. That average carcass weight (also known as the hot hanging weight) is taken when an animal has been partially butchered (its head, hide, internal organs, and intestinal tract removed), but the remaining meat and bones haven't yet been chilled.

Bouvry processes about 5,000 bison a year. Anne oversees identification and traceability. Just like at Prairie Meats (the provincial slaughterhouse where we get a few of our bison processed for local freezer sales), the bison are killed with one shot, this time from a .223 rifle.

"The guys are trained so it's one bullet and it's done," says Anne matter-of-factly. She grades the carcasses. The ideal meat is firm, and bright red (dark meat is a sign of stress), and has about $\frac{1}{16}$ to $\frac{1}{4}$ inch (2 to 6 millimeters) of white/amber fat. Bison meat doesn't really marble.

Anne's not too interested in the wholesale/retail end of things. "Once they're dead, it's not my part anymore," she says with a shrug.

The Europe-bound meat flies daily to France and is then shipped to Germany, Italy, and Switzerland. The Europeans prefer upscale cuts like tenderloin, striploin, rib eye, and sirloin. It's too expensive to ship ground meat (all the trim is sent to Bouvry's Quebec plant for grinding), but heart and tongue are sometimes requested.

The Quebec-bound meat is sold mainly as steaks or roast to restaurants, and through two major distributors, including Bouvry's brand, Viande Richelieu Meat. Viande Richelieu was founded in 1986 to breed and process bison, horse, elk, and beef.

"Pretty much all I eat is bison, horse, and lamb—I don't eat beef, chicken, or pork," says Anne.

Why not, I ask.

"I work in the meat industry," she explains. "With horse and bison, I know there are no growth hormones, and no additives or antibiotics in their feed."

We talk for a bit about cooking bison (see Anne's bourguignon on page 145), and then Anne invites me to visit the farm. "I couldn't go back to cattle," she declares. "Once you taste bison, you can't do anything else. It's fun."

Anne loves the wild and stubborn nature of bison. She has learned to be patient and never push them. Twice a day, she walks her dog Gadjo through fields full of heifers. Gadjo, an Australian sheepdog/border collie cross, has learned to not herd the bison.

"Your heifers are so dangerous—I have to be careful," Anne says. It's a huge compliment. She means there's a lot of wild left in our bison.

A few weeks later, Rick and I drive to Bouvry's 160-acre (65-hectare) farm with our two younger kids in tow. It's the first time Rick and Anne meet, since they make their deals by phone.

We pass by some "little boys" in the corrals and drive through various pastures to see some heifers. It's lush and green and Rick's pleasantly surprised. "It's a nice setup—they

have lots of room." There are exactly 772 bison here today. He recognizes a few of ours by their tags.

The bison eye us curiously but keep their distance. "It's safe," Anne assures us. "They're not going to come close. The most danger is the poo."

We try to dodge the "bison chips," glad that these girls have never calved and so have nothing to protect.

"They're really playful, aren't they?" says Rick. "Cattle are kind of boring." He and Anne chitchat about bison, and I examine the oats the bison are helping themselves to from self-feeders. We don't feed oats to our bison, but these guys seem pleased to have the option. Back at the ranch, Rick and Anne wander off to examine Bouvry's handling system.

Soon we pile back into the car, glad to see the bison doing well and being cared for by someone as smart and compassionate as Anne. (We don't know it yet, but Anne is about to leave Bouvry.)

"Well, that makes me feel better," says Rick. "The buffs are pretty happy here."

CHAPTER 3

Steaks

Here are my nine tips for perfect steaks:

1. Cut steaks at least 1 inch thick (or even 1½ inches).
2. Let them sit at room temperature for 30 minutes to 1 hour so they cook evenly.
3. Pat steaks dry with paper towels before cooking.
4. Cook them in a preheated cast-iron skillet over medium heat, or barbecue them. (Ideally, you should preheat your skillet for 30 minutes to get it nice and hot. But if you are short on time, a minimum of 15 minutes will suffice.)
5. Most steaks need about 4 minutes per side, but that's a rough rule of thumb that will change depending on the cut, thickness, meat temperature, cooking temperature, and type of skillet used. I cook the first side a little longer, to get a nice crust on the bottom. I cook the second side until tiny red/pink juices dot the surface.
6. I like my steaks rare or medium-rare, but you can go as far as medium. If you cook beyond this, the bison will be tough and dry. There are many conflicting meat temperature guidelines out there. I favor the temperatures used by chefs for steaks.
    - Rare is 135°F.
    - Medium-rare is 145°F.
    - Medium is 155°F.
7. Here's the catch: You should undercook by about five degrees because the temperature will continue to rise while the steaks rest.
    - For rare, cook to 130°F.
    - For medium-rare, cook to 140°F.
    - For medium, cook to 150°F.
8. Use a digital thermometer.
9. Let steaks rest on a cutting board, loosely covered with foil, for 10 minutes before slicing so the temperature rises slightly and the juices redistribute instead of spilling out.

I cook steaks on the stove, and they are every bit as good as grilled. I watched Toronto chef Roger Romberg, from George Brown College's culinary management program, cook rib eyes this way at the *Toronto Star* test kitchen in 2001 for my food colleague Amy Pataki. We had an abysmal island with eight countertop electric burners that barely worked, yet the steaks were stunning. I've used this method, with a few tweaks, ever since. This method is flexible—you can take shortcuts when bringing the steak to room temperature and preheating the skillet. Having a thick steak, however, is nonnegotiable. Demand 1 to 1½ inches so that you'll have time to brown the outside and create a crust while keeping the center moist and rare.

Cast-Iron Skillet Bison Steak with Caramelized Onions

Makes 1 steak

Let the steak stand at room temperature for 1 hour. Pat dry with paper towels. Season generously with salt and pepper. Rub all over with oil. (I oil my steaks instead of the skillet; this prevents the skillet from smoking while preheating.)

Meanwhile, heat a cast-iron skillet over medium for 15 to 30 minutes. Add the steak, presentation side down. Cook for 4 minutes or until the underside is golden brown, reducing the heat if the meat cooks too fast and starts to blacken. Flip using tongs. Cook to rare or medium-rare, monitoring how the other side browns and watching for when pink/red juices appear on the surface. This will take about 2 to 3 minutes.

Transfer the steak to a cutting board. Let it stand, loosely covered with foil, for 10 minutes so it can redistribute and reabsorb its juices. (The juices move to the surface while cooking and will spill out if the steak is cut immediately.) If desired, serve topped with caramelized onions.

1 bison rib-eye or other steak, 1 to 1½ inches thick

Kosher salt

Freshly ground black pepper

Extra-virgin olive oil

Caramelized Onions, to taste (optional, see p. 84)

It drives me crazy when I see recipes for "caramelized" onions that only call for a brief cooking time. Ten minutes will get you fried onions, in my humble opinion. Thirty minutes will get you gorgeously cooked onions. But you need to devote about an hour to coaxing your onions to caramelize. Serve these warm or cold on burgers and steaks. They're great tucked into sandwiches as well.

Caramelized Onions

Makes about 1¼ cups

Put the onions in a large nonstick skillet over medium-high heat. Drizzle with 3 tablespoons of the oil. Cook, stirring, for 10 minutes, until the onions just start to burn. Turn the heat down to medium. Cook for 20 minutes, stirring often and adding the remaining 1 tablespoon of oil if needed. Reduce the heat to medium-low. Cook, stirring, for 30 minutes, until you have a small pile of caramelized onions.

I like my onions like this, but you may want to stir in a little sugar and balsamic vinegar at this point to round out the flavors.

Refrigerate, covered, for up to 5 days.

2 lb yellow, red, white, and/or sweet onions (about 4 large), halved and thinly sliced (about 8 cups)

3 to 4 Tbsp extra-virgin olive oil, divided

Pinch granulated sugar (optional)

Splash aged balsamic vinegar (optional)

I adore this Thai-spiced marmalade from Ohio chef Brandt Evans; it's one of my favorite ways to doll up steaks. "We live in such a melting-pot world," he says. "I always like to combine different cultures when cooking. I knew with bison being so lean and a bigger 'beefy' flavor, I needed to come up with something that would stand along with it and not overpower or underpower it. When I cook or design menus/recipes, I try to build flavors like a staircase—at every step you taste another flavor that just adds to the dish." Brandt owns BKM Hospitality and Pura Vida by Brandt restaurant in Cleveland, and is a partner in Blue Canyon Kitchen and Tavern in Twinsburg.

Bison Steaks with Thai Red Curry, Coconut + Onion Marmalade

Makes 4 servings

For the marmalade, in a medium saucepan over medium-high, heat the oil. Add the onions and garlic. Cook, stirring, for 10 minutes until soft. Add the sugar, coconut milk, and curry paste. Whisk until the paste is dissolved. Cook, stirring frequently, until you have a thick, glaze-like consistency, about 20 to 30 minutes, lowering the heat as needed. The sauce should coat the back of a spoon. Remove from the heat. Stir in the rosemary. Serve warm or refrigerate and serve cold. (Makes about 2 cups.)

For the steaks, let the meat stand at room temperature for 30 minutes to 1 hour. Pat dry with paper towels. Season generously with salt and pepper. Rub with oil.

Meanwhile, heat a large cast-iron skillet over medium for 15 to 30 minutes. Add the steaks. Cook for 4 minutes, until the undersides are browned. Flip. Cook for about 3 minutes for medium-rare, or to desired doneness. Transfer the steaks to a plate or cutting board. Cover loosely with foil. Let the meat rest for 10 minutes before serving.

Serve the steaks topped with a generous dollop of marmalade, or pass the marmalade separately.

MARMALADE:

2 Tbsp extra-virgin olive oil

1 lb red onions (about 2 medium), halved and thinly sliced

3 cloves garlic, minced

¾ cup granulated sugar

1 (14 oz) can coconut milk

1 Tbsp Thai red curry paste

2 tsp finely chopped fresh rosemary

STEAKS:

4 bison steaks, each about 1 inch thick

Kosher salt

Freshly ground black pepper

Extra-virgin olive oil

Chimichurri is a spiced parsley condiment that's popular in Argentina and Uruguay with grilled meat. This version comes from CHARCUT Roast House in Calgary (charcut.com), thanks to chef/owner Connie DeSousa and chef John Jackson. This sauce is also delicious slathered on CHARCUT Roast House's Bison Heart (p. 204), Bison Puffs (p. 54), or any bison roast or steak.

Bison Steaks with Chimichurri Sauce

Makes 4 servings

For the chimichurri, in a mini or regular food processor, combine the parsley, garlic, rosemary, oregano, red wine vinegar, water, salt, pepper, and chili flakes. Pulse until roughly chopped. With the motor running, drizzle in the oil and process until smooth. Transfer to a small bowl. Serve immediately or refrigerate, covered, for several days. (Makes about ¾ cup.)

For the steaks, let the meat stand at room temperature for 30 minutes to 1 hour. Pat dry with paper towels. Season generously with salt and pepper. Rub with oil.

Meanwhile, heat a large cast-iron skillet over medium for 15 to 30 minutes. Add the steaks. Cook for 4 minutes, until the undersides are browned. Flip. Cook for about 3 minutes for medium-rare, or to desired doneness. Transfer the steaks to a plate or cutting board. Cover loosely with foil. Let the meat rest for 10 minutes before serving slathered with chimichurri.

CHIMICHURRI:

1 cup packed flat-leaf parsley leaves

2 cloves garlic, chopped

2 sprigs fresh rosemary, chopped

½ tsp chopped fresh oregano

2 Tbsp red wine vinegar

2 Tbsp water

½ tsp kosher salt

½ tsp freshly ground black pepper

½ tsp red chili flakes

½ cup extra-virgin olive oil

STEAKS:

4 bison steaks, each about 1 inch thick

Kosher salt

Freshly ground black pepper

Extra-virgin olive oil

I'm usually a purist and like my steaks unadorned, with just enough salt, pepper, and olive oil to help form a crust, but I make an exception for this Latin flavor combination adapted from a recipe by American restaurateur Isabel Cruz (isabelscantina.com).

Chipotle-Lime Bison Steaks

Makes 4 to 6 servings

In a medium mixing bowl, combine the lime juice, chipotle purée, brown sugar, and salt. Whisk in the oil.

Place the steaks in a large resealable plastic bag. Add half of the chipotle-lime mixture, turning the steaks to coat well. Refrigerate, turning the bag occasionally, for 4 hours to overnight. Cover the remaining chipotle-lime mixture and refrigerate separately, to use as a condiment.

To cook, remove the steaks from the marinade and let them stand at room temperature for 30 minutes. Discard the marinade. Pat the steaks dry with paper towels.

Meanwhile, heat a large cast-iron skillet over medium for 15 to 30 minutes. Add the steaks. Cook for 4 minutes to form a crust, and then flip with tongs. Cook for about 3 minutes for medium-rare, or to desired doneness.

Transfer the steaks to a cutting board and let them stand, loosely covered with foil, for 10 minutes. Serve whole, or cut into thick slices and arrange on a platter.

Pass the reserved chipotle-lime sauce separately, stirring in the cilantro just before serving.

Juice of 4 limes

3 Tbsp puréed canned chipotle chilies packed in adobo sauce (see Cooking Tip, p. 32)

3 Tbsp light brown sugar

1 tsp kosher salt

1 cup extra-virgin olive oil

4 small bison steaks (such as top sirloin), each 1 inch thick

2 Tbsp chopped cilantro

Steak and chocolate sauce is a popular pairing, but there are all kinds of needlessly complicated recipes out there. The simpler the better, I say. This version is adapted from a recipe by Montreal chef and Food Network star Nadia Giosia (bitchinlifestyle.tv). The better your balsamic vinegar and chocolate, the better your results. If you live near a chocolatier, see what kind of dark chocolate they have. Otherwise, most supermarkets sell Lindt brand dark chocolate bars (go for 70, 85, or 90 percent cacao).

Bison Steaks with Chocolate-Balsamic Sauce

Makes 4 servings

Let the steaks rest at room temperature for 30 minutes to 1 hour. Pat dry with paper towels. Season generously with salt and pepper. Rub all over with oil.

Heat a large cast-iron skillet over medium for 15 to 30 minutes. Add the steaks. Cook for 4 minutes. Flip. Cook for about 3 minutes for medium-rare, or to desired doneness. Transfer the steaks to a plate. Cover loosely with foil. Let stand for 10 minutes.

Meanwhile, in a small saucepan over medium-high heat, bring the balsamic vinegar and maple syrup to a gentle boil. Reduce the heat to medium. Simmer for 10 minutes or until slightly thickened. Remove from the heat. Whisk in the chocolate until melted.

Serve the steaks drizzled with the sauce, or pass the sauce separately.

4 small bison steaks (such as tenderloin or top sirloin), each about 1 inch thick

Kosher salt

Freshly ground black pepper

Extra-virgin olive oil

½ cup aged balsamic vinegar

½ cup pure maple syrup

2 Tbsp finely grated dark chocolate (70% to 90% cacao)

The funny thing about whisky/whiskey is that I can't bear it in cocktails but adore it in sauces. It pairs beautifully with a bison steak. Bourbon (an American whiskey) is a little sweeter, Scotch (a Scottish whisky) is a tad smoky, and rye (a Canadian whisky) is yeasty—you can use whatever you have in your liquor cabinet.

Bison Steaks with Boozy Mustard Sauce

Makes 4 servings

Let the steaks rest at room temperature for 30 minutes to 1 hour. Pat dry with paper towels. Season generously with salt and pepper. Rub all over with oil.

Heat a large cast-iron skillet over medium for 15 to 30 minutes. Add the steaks. Cook for 4 minutes, until a nice crust forms. Flip. Cook for about 3 minutes for medium-rare, or to desired doneness. Transfer the meat to a cutting board. Let the steaks stand, loosely covered with foil, for 10 minutes.

Meanwhile, for the mustard sauce, in a small saucepan over medium-high, heat the oil. Add the shallots and garlic. Cook, stirring, for 5 minutes to soften. Add the whiskey. Boil for 5 minutes. Add the stock or water and grainy mustard. Boil for 10 minutes. Stir in the butter and any accumulated juices from the steaks. Cook, stirring, for 1 minute or until the butter melts. Season to taste with salt and pepper.

Serve the steaks with the sauce passed separately.

4 bison steaks, each about 1 inch thick
Kosher salt
Freshly ground black pepper
Extra-virgin olive oil

MUSTARD SAUCE:
1 Tbsp extra-virgin olive oil
2 small shallots, minced
1 clove garlic, minced
½ cup whiskey (such as bourbon, Scotch, or rye)
1 cup bison or beef stock or water
2 Tbsp grainy mustard
3 Tbsp unsalted butter
Kosher salt
Freshly ground black pepper

Chef Michael Paley loves bison, especially tenderloins, tongue, tail, brisket, and chuck. Luckily, his bosses, Laura Lee Brown and Steve Wilson, raise bison. He created this dish in 2006 while working at Proof on Main in Louisville, Kentucky. Michael is now executive chef of Metropole at 21c Museum Hotel in Cincinnati (metropoleonwalnut.com), and chef/partner of Garage Bar pizzeria (garageonmarket.com) in Louisville. This dish is inspired by the classic Bistecca Fiorentina from Tuscany, a T-bone simply seasoned with good-quality salt, cooked over wood coals, served rare to medium-rare, and garnished with aged balsamic vinegar.

Bison Steaks with Rosemary Oil + Smoked Salt on Buttery Leeks

Makes 2 servings

Let the steaks stand, loosely covered with wax paper, at room temperature for 30 minutes to 1 hour. Pat dry with paper towels. Season the steaks with salt and pepper. Rub with oil.

Heat a large cast-iron skillet over medium for 15 to 30 minutes. Add the steaks. Cook for 4 minutes, until a nice crust forms on the undersides. Flip. Cook for about 3 minutes for medium-rare, or to desired doneness. Transfer to a cutting board. Let the steaks rest, loosely covered with foil, for 10 minutes.

Meanwhile, in a medium saucepan over medium heat, melt the butter. Add the leeks. Season to taste with salt and pepper. Reduce the heat to low. Cook, stirring, until soft and buttery, about 10 to 15 minutes.

At the same time, in a small skillet over low heat, warm the 2 tablespoons of olive oil and the rosemary sprigs for 10 minutes to infuse the oil with flavor.

To serve, divide the leeks between 2 plates. Place 1 steak on each leek pile. Garnish each with a drizzle of rosemary olive oil, a drizzle of balsamic vinegar, a rosemary sprig, and a sprinkling of smoked salt.

2 bison tenderloin steaks or other bison steaks, each about 1 inch thick

Kosher salt

Freshly ground black pepper

Extra-virgin olive oil for the steak + 2 Tbsp for the rosemary oil

2 Tbsp unsalted butter

3 leeks, white and light green parts only, washed, dried, and diced

2 sprigs fresh rosemary + more for garnish

Aged balsamic vinegar, for drizzling

Flaky smoked sea salt, for garnish

" I wanted to do a bone-in signature steak for the restaurant, and our owners own a bison farm in Goshen, Kentucky, so I had firsthand access to fresh bison—the kind of access most people don't have because bison was, and still is, I believe, a niche product as compared to beef." —Michael Paley

This gorgeous bison meal won Jean-Francois Daigle the Canadian Regional title at the ninth annual S. Pellegrino Almost Famous Chef Competition in 2011, while he was at George Brown College's Chef School in Toronto. Rich bison tenderloin sits atop creamy apple-parsnip purée and is surrounded by a chunky vegetable sauce.

Honey-Seared Bison Tenderloin with Apple-Parsnip Purée

Makes 4 servings

For the vegetable sauce, in a medium saucepan over high heat, bring the stock, wine, carrots, onions, celery, bay leaves, and pepper to a boil. Reduce the heat to medium-high. Simmer briskly until the mixture is reduced to 2½ cups, about 10 to 15 minutes. Discard the bay leaves. Reduce the heat to low and cover the sauce to keep warm.

Meanwhile, for the tenderloins, let the meat stand at room temperature for 30 minutes to 1 hour. Pat dry with paper towels. Sprinkle with salt and pepper. Rub with oil.

Preheat the oven to 425°F.

Heat a large cast-iron skillet over medium for 15 to 30 minutes. Add the tenderloins. Sear for 2 minutes per side, and then drizzle with the honey and sprinkle with the thyme. Insert an ovenproof digital thermometer into the meat.

Transfer the skillet to the oven. Roast to 130°F for rare, 140°F for medium-rare, or 150°F for medium. Transfer the meat to a cutting board and let it stand, loosely covered with foil, for 10 minutes. The temperature will rise about 5 degrees.

To serve, spoon some Apple-Parsnip Purée onto the center of each of 4 plates. Top each with 1 tenderloin. Spoon the vegetable sauce around the meat on each plate.

VEGETABLE SAUCE:

2 cups bison or beef stock

⅔ cup dry red wine

1 cup peeled and finely diced carrots

1 cup finely diced yellow onions

¾ cup diced celery

2 bay leaves

1 tsp cracked black pepper

BISON:

4 bison tenderloin steaks, each about 4 ounces

Kosher salt

Freshly ground black pepper

Extra-virgin olive oil

2 Tbsp honey

1 Tbsp chopped fresh thyme

Apple-Parsnip Purée (optional, see opposite page)

This sweet root and fruit mash, from young chef Jean-Francois Daigle, is a welcome change from potatoes.

Apple-Parsnip Purée

Makes 4 servings

Bring a large saucepan of water to boil over high heat. Add the parsnips and cover. Cook for 15 minutes or until the parsnips are tender. Add the apples. Reduce the heat to low and cover. Simmer for 10 minutes or until the apples and parsnips are very tender. Drain well. Purée in a food processor until smooth, or mash well by hand. Whisk in the cream and mustard. Season to taste with salt and pepper. Cover and keep warm.

1 lb parsnips, peeled and chopped

1 lb apples (about 3 large), peeled, cored, and chopped

2 Tbsp whipping cream, warmed

2 tsp Dijon mustard

Kosher salt

Freshly ground black pepper

Yellowknife chef Pierre LePage prepared this showstopper of a dish during a tourism event in Toronto. If this combination is too rich for your taste, the herbed meat is perfect on its own. Any leftover Gorgonzola butter is stunning on baked potatoes.

Rosemary-Crusted Bison Tenderloin with Gorgonzola Butter

Makes 4 servings

For the Gorgonzola butter, in a small bowl, stir together the butter, cheese, garlic, and shallot until well blended. On a large piece of plastic wrap, form the butter mixture into a log, about 4 inches long. Wrap well. Refrigerate for at least 1 hour, until solid. When ready to use, cut into 4 coins.

For the steaks, let the bison stand at room temperature for 30 minutes to 1 hour. Pat dry with paper towels.

In a small bowl, combine the rosemary and pepper.

Preheat the oven to 425°F.

Heat a large cast-iron or ovenproof skillet over medium-high. Add the oil, and then the tenderloin. Brown, 2 minutes per side. Transfer the steaks to a cutting board. Let the meat stand for 5 minutes. Brush all over with the mustard. Rub all over with the rosemary mixture.

Return the meat to the skillet and insert an ovenproof digital thermometer in the thickest part of the meat. Roast until the thermometer reads 130°F for rare, 140°F for medium-rare, or 150°F for medium, about 6 to 10 minutes.

Transfer the steaks to a cutting board, cover loosely with foil, and let stand for 10 minutes so the temperature will rise by about 5 degrees.

Serve each steak with a coin of Gorgonzola butter on top.

GORGONZOLA BUTTER:

2 Tbsp unsalted butter, at room temperature

2 oz crumbled Gorgonzola cheese, at room temperature

1 clove garlic, minced

1 Tbsp minced shallot

STEAKS:

4 bison tenderloin steaks, each about 1 inch thick

½ cup fresh rosemary leaves, chopped

2 Tbsp cracked black pepper

2 Tbsp extra-virgin olive oil

¼ cup Dijon mustard

Calgary chef Andrew Winfield believes bison flank is the perfect cut for his flavorful marinade, which uses local hot peppers and green onions from his River Café (river-cafe.com) culinary garden. "[Jerk] is not something that a lot of people work with because they're afraid of the chilies and the hot spices of the Caribbean," he says. "But Canada is such a melting pot." To show off the tenderness and flavor of the cut, flank steak is best cooked to medium-rare and thinly sliced against the grain. The chef would serve this with grilled peaches, sautéed chanterelles, and a lightly dressed salad.

River Café's Jerk-Marinated Bison Flank Steak

Makes 4 servings

For the jerk marinade, in a blender, combine the green onions, sweet onion, pepper, lime flesh, ginger, brown sugar, soy sauce, olive oil and camelina, canola, or grapeseed oil, allspice, and salt. Purée until smooth.

In a resealable plastic bag, combine the steak pieces and jerk marinade. Rub the marinade all over the meat. Seal the bag, pushing out the air. Refrigerate for at least 3 hours to overnight.

To cook, remove the steak pieces from the marinade. If time allows, let the meat stand at room temperature for 30 minutes to 1 hour. Preheat the barbecue to high. Cook the steak, uncovered, for 1 to 2 minutes per side, for medium-rare. Alternately, heat a large cast-iron skillet over medium for 15 to 30 minutes. Cook the steak for 1 to 2 minutes per side, or to desired doneness.

Let the steak pieces stand on a cutting board, loosely covered with foil, for 10 minutes before thinly slicing against the grain.

JERK MARINADE:

2 green onions

6 Tbsp chopped sweet onion (such as Vidalia)

½ Scotch bonnet or habanero pepper, seeded if desired

1 lime, peeled

1½ tsp peeled and minced ginger

2 Tbsp light brown sugar

1½ Tbsp light soy sauce

1 Tbsp extra-virgin olive oil

1 Tbsp camelina oil, first-pressed canola oil, or grapeseed oil

2 tsp whole allspice

1½ tsp kosher salt

STEAK:

1 bison flank steak (about 1 to 1½ lb), cut into 4 pieces

" I love bison. It's a sweeter-style meat. I find it strange that people talk about the gamey flavors because I don't taste that."
—Andrew Winfield

While chef Oliver Bartsch was employed at Rideau Hall to cook for the governor general and visiting dignitaries, he made this dish for the Showcase of Culinary Riches at the 2004 Expo Québec. He went on to cook for the prime minister at 24 Sussex Drive and is now the chef for the Supreme Court of Canada. Sumac is a tart and fruity dried spice that's popular in Middle Eastern cooking. (No, it's not from the poisonous sumac shrub.) The sauce cooks away but the intense flavor remains intact.

Sumac-Rubbed Bison Flank Steak

Makes about 4 servings

In a small mixing bowl or measuring cup, stir together the sumac, chili powder, sugar, onion powder, garlic powder, allspice, salt, and pepper. Add the oil, soy sauce, and mustard. Stir into a thick paste. Rub all over the steak. Let the meat stand for 1 hour at room temperature. Alternately, refrigerate, covered, overnight.

Heat a large cast-iron skillet over medium for 15 to 30 minutes. Add the steak. Cook for 2 minutes. Flip. Cook for 2 minutes for medium-rare, or to desired doneness. Transfer to a cutting board and let stand, loosely covered with foil, for 10 minutes. Cut the steak against the grain in thin slices.

2 Tbsp ground sumac

1 tsp chili powder

1 tsp granulated sugar

½ tsp onion powder

½ tsp garlic powder

½ tsp ground allspice

½ tsp kosher salt

½ tsp freshly ground black pepper

2 Tbsp extra-virgin olive oil

1 Tbsp soy sauce

1 Tbsp Dijon mustard

1 bison flank steak (about 1 to 1½ lb), cut about ¾ inch thick, silver skin discarded, and fat trimmed

" Bison is part of our heritage, our culture. I just feel, as a chef who's promoting Canadian foods, that it's normal to be using it. Bison is sort of this exotic meat. It has a wilder flavor but it's not quite as wild as venison. The flavor is just so incredible. I love it." —Oliver Bartsch

Back at the ranch in 2008 and 2009 while on maternity leave, I spent a lot of time trolling the Internet (we still had dial-up!) for bison recipes. I got the idea for these pretty pinwheels from D'Artagnan (dartagnan.com), an upscale meat purveyor from the United States. Smoked cheese is one of my favorite flavor boosters.

Bison Flank Steak Stuffed with Roasted Peppers + Smoked Cheese

Makes 4 to 6 servings

Preheat the oven to 400°F.

If your butcher won't butterfly your steak, do it yourself with a long, sharp knife. Start on the long side of the flank and begin slicing the meat in half lengthwise but not all the way through. Cut to about ¾ inch from the other side. Open the steak like a book and flatten it. Pat the meat dry with paper towels.

Season the meat all over with salt and pepper. Sprinkle with the garlic and herbs. Lay the red peppers on the right third of the meat. Cover with the cheese slices. Roll up with the grain, starting at the right edge. Close the roll with short metal skewers or kitchen twine along the roll every 1½ inches. Turn the ends under and secure with skewers.

In a small bowl, whisk together the mustard, oil, and Worcestershire sauce.

Place the steak roll in a large cast-iron skillet. Brush with the mustard mixture. Insert an ovenproof digital thermometer into the center of the roll. Transfer the skillet to the oven. Cook to 130°F for rare, 140°F for medium-rare, or 150°F for medium, about 12 to 18 minutes, turning twice and brushing with the mustard mixture each time.

Transfer the steak to a cutting board. Let it stand for 10 minutes before removing the skewers or strings. Cut the meat into 1-inch slices.

1 bison flank steak (about 1 to 1½ lb), butterflied

Kosher salt

Freshly ground black pepper

3 large cloves garlic, minced

¼ cup chopped fresh herbs (such as basil, thyme, or oregano)

2 roasted whole red bell peppers (from a jar)

3½ oz smoked Gouda or smoked cheddar, thinly sliced

¼ cup Dijon mustard

1 Tbsp extra-virgin olive oil

1 tsp Worcestershire sauce

"When it comes to bison, one of my favorite cuts is skirt steak," reveals Timothy Wasylko, personal chef to Prime Minister Stephen Harper at 24 Sussex Drive. "It is reasonably priced, and a very good yield, and has a rich, deep flavor profile." This is a dish that he makes at home. It can be hard to get skirt steak (there isn't a lot of it on a bison), so you may substitute flank.

Stuffed Bison Skirt Steak with Charred Green Onion Pesto

Makes 4 to 6 servings

In a small saucepan over low heat, combine the garlic cloves and oil. Cook until golden brown, about 15 minutes. Reserve the garlic and the oil in separate bowls. When the garlic cools slightly, mash it into a paste with a fork.

Meanwhile, let the steak stand at room temperature for 30 minutes to 1 hour. Pat dry with paper towels. With a sharp knife, remove any silver skin or fat from the meat. Using a meat mallet (or the bottom of a heavy skillet), pound the steak gently until it is ¾ inch thick. Season with the salt and pepper. Spread the mashed garlic evenly around the steak. Sprinkle with the pine nuts. Dot with the goat cheese. Scatter with the arugula. Working lengthwise, lift and pull the long sides together. Firmly tie in 6 spots with kitchen twine to create a log.

Preheat the oven to 400°F.

In a large cast-iron or ovenproof skillet over medium-high, heat 1 tablespoon of the reserved garlic oil. Add the roast. Cook until browned all over, about 6 minutes. Insert an ovenproof digital thermometer into the meat.

Transfer the skillet to the oven. Bake until the temperature reaches 130°F for rare, 140°F for medium-rare, or 150°F for medium, about 15 to 20 minutes. Transfer the steak to a cutting board. Cover loosely with foil. Let it stand for 10 minutes so the temperature can rise about 5 degrees. Remove the string. Slice against the grain into 1-inch pieces.

Serve the steak drizzled with the pesto if desired.

6 cloves garlic, peeled

3 Tbsp canola oil

1 to 1½ lb bison skirt steak

¼ tsp kosher salt

¼ tsp cracked black pepper

3 Tbsp pine nuts, toasted

¼ to ½ cup crumbled chèvre (fresh goat cheese)

½ cup baby arugula

Charred Green Onion Pesto (optional, see opposite page)

When most people think of pesto, they think of the basil version. Not Timothy Wasylko, personal chef to Prime Minister Stephen Harper. He goes supergreen with charred green onions, basil, parsley, and mint.

Charred Green Onion Pesto

Makes about ¾ cup

Heat a large nonstick skillet or grill pan over medium-high.

In a bowl, toss the green onions and canola oil. Transfer to the pan and cook until slightly charred, about 5 minutes. Transfer to a blender. Allow to cool for 5 minutes. Add the basil, parsley, mint, garlic, lemon zest, olive oil, and chili paste. Season to taste with salt and pepper. Purée. If not serving immediately, refrigerate until ready to use.

1 bunch green onions, trimmed and halved

2 Tbsp canola oil

¼ cup fresh basil leaves

¼ cup flat-leaf parsley leaves

¼ cup mint leaves

2 large cloves garlic, peeled and smashed

Finely grated zest of 1 lemon

¼ cup extra-virgin olive oil

1 tsp sambal oelek or other Asian chili paste

Kosher salt

Freshly ground black pepper

This is my "everything but the kitchen sink" meat-and-veg meal. It's a tribute to ingredients that I always have lying around. This makes a quick and satisfying dinner for two.

Bison Skirt Steak Meal

Makes 2 servings

For the meat, let the steak stand at room temperature for 30 minutes to 1 hour. Pat dry with paper towels. In a bowl, mix the salt, pepper, and cumin. Rub all over the meat. Rub with oil.

Heat a cast-iron skillet over medium for 15 to 30 minutes. Cook the steak for 2 minutes. Flip. Cook for 1 to 2 minutes, depending on the thickness of the meat. Transfer the steak to a cutting board and let it stand, loosely covered, for 10 minutes before thinly slicing.

For the veg, in a large skillet over medium-high, heat the oil. Add the onions, bell peppers, and jalapeno. Cook, stirring, until soft, about 7 to 10 minutes. Stir in the cilantro.

For the sauce, in a small bowl, stir together the sour cream and horseradish. Season to taste with salt and pepper.

To serve, divide the steak and veg over 2 plates. Pass the sauce separately.

MEAT:

1 bison skirt steak (about 12 oz)

1 tsp kosher salt

½ tsp freshly ground black pepper

½ tsp ground cumin

Extra-virgin olive oil

VEG:

3 Tbsp extra-virgin olive oil

2 medium yellow onions, halved and thinly sliced

2 red bell peppers, thinly sliced

1 jalapeno, minced with seeds

½ cup cilantro leaves

HORSERADISH-CREAM SAUCE:

¼ cup sour cream

1 Tbsp drained prepared hot horseradish

Kosher salt

Freshly ground black pepper

This unusually flavored braised dish is an all-time favorite of Mario Fiorucci, cofounder of the Healthy Butcher in Toronto (healthybutcher.com). "Most people automatically assume that bison, like other red meat, must be paired with red wine," says Mario. "On the contrary, white wine works wonders to bring out the delicate flavor of quality red meat." Serve this over mashed potatoes or sweet potatoes.

Bison Blade Steaks Braised in White Wine with Figs + Raisins

Makes 4 to 6 servings

Generously season the steaks with salt and pepper.

Heat a large pot over medium-high and add the oil and butter. In two batches, sear the meat for 2 minutes per side. Transfer to a plate. Add the onions, carrots, celery, and garlic to the pot. Cook, stirring, for 10 minutes. Add the wine and cook until the liquid is reduced by half.

Return the meat and any accumulated juices to the pot. Add the stock. It should barely cover the meat. Bring to a boil over high heat. Add the thyme and bay leaves. Cover and cook on the stove over medium-low heat, or in an oven preheated to 300°F, for 2 hours. Strain, returning the meat and liquid to the pot, and discarding the vegetables. Add the raisins and figs to the pot. Return to a bare simmer on the stove, or return the pot to the oven. Cook until the meat becomes fork-tender, about 1 to 2 hours (it will get tough before it falls apart).

Strain, reserving the steaks, raisins, and figs. The meat will have fallen apart into chunks and smaller pieces. If needed, chop the steaks as desired into serving portions.

If you wish, put the braising liquid into a medium saucepan and boil over high heat until thickened and reduced to desired consistency, about 10 to 15 minutes.

Serve the steak with the raisins and figs. Drizzle with the reduced sauce.

Boneless bison blade steaks (about 2 lb total), patted dry

Kosher salt

Freshly ground black pepper

1 tsp extra-virgin olive oil

1 tsp unsalted butter

3 medium yellow onions, chopped

2 carrots, peeled and chopped

2 stalks celery, chopped

6 cloves garlic, peeled

2 cups white wine

4 cups bison or beef stock

¼ bunch fresh thyme

2 bay leaves

½ cup sultana or golden raisins

8 dried figs, stemmed

I went to the Calgary Stampede in 2013 just to watch Andrew Stevens, corporate chef of the Vintage Group (vintagegroup.ca), make these grilled flank sandwiches with horseradish mayo and charred pepper vinaigrette. I asked for seconds (and thirds). Yes, they're a little more work than most sandwiches but they're so worth the effort.

Calgary Stampede Bison Sandwiches

Makes 6

In a large resealable plastic bag, combine the tamari or soy sauce, olive oil, Worcestershire sauce, lemon juice, garlic, and pepper. Stir well. Add the steak. Seal the bag. Refrigerate overnight or for up to 24 hours.

To cook the steak, remove the meat from the plastic bag and pat dry with paper towels. Discard the marinade. Let the meat stand at room temperature for 30 minutes to 1 hour.

Heat a grill pan over medium-high. Cook the steak for about 2 minutes per side for medium-rare. Transfer the steak to a cutting board. Let it stand, loosely covered with foil, for 5 minutes (the temperature will rise slightly) before thinly slicing against the grain.

To assemble the sandwiches, spread the insides of the rolls, top and bottom, with Horseradish Mayo. On the bun bottoms, pile some steak, Charred Red Pepper Vinaigrette, and arugula, and then cover with the bun tops.

6 Tbsp tamari or light soy sauce

2 Tbsp extra-virgin olive oil

1½ Tbsp Worcestershire sauce

1 Tbsp fresh lemon juice

2 cloves garlic, minced

1 tsp freshly ground black pepper

2 lb bison flank steak

6 ciabatta or other sandwich rolls, toasted if desired

Horseradish Mayo (see opposite page)

Charred Red Pepper Vinaigrette (see opposite page)

Baby arugula

" Some bison are finished on grass, some are finished on grain. It's a safe and wonderful meat for your family. It's basically a chemical-free meat." —Andrew Stevens

Sure, you can simply put storebought creamed horseradish right onto your sandwiches, but as Calgary chef Andrew Stevens shows here, if you step up your cooking game just a bit, you can create a memorable horseradish-cream sauce.

Horseradish Mayo

Makes about 1 cup

In a small bowl, combine the mayonnaise, green onion, horseradish, lemon zest, and lemon juice. Season to taste with salt and pepper. Cover and refrigerate until ready to use.

1 cup mayonnaise

1 Tbsp chopped green onion

2 tsp drained prepared horseradish

Finely grated zest and juice of ½ a lemon

Kosher salt

Freshly ground black pepper

This isn't liquid like a typical vinaigrette. Think of Andrew's creation as a chunky, vinaigrette-seasoned ode to red peppers. He roasts his own red peppers, but I've taken a shortcut and bought mine.

Charred Red Pepper Vinaigrette

Makes about 1½ cups

In a medium bowl, combine the red peppers, garlic, basil, oil, and red wine vinegar. Season to taste with salt and pepper. Cover and let stand for 30 minutes at room temperature so the flavors can blend. If not serving immediately, the vinaigrette can be refrigerated for several days, until ready to use.

3 roasted red bell peppers (from a jar), finely diced

2 cloves garlic, minced

10 fresh basil leaves, thinly sliced

3 Tbsp extra-virgin olive oil

1 Tbsp red wine vinegar

Kosher salt

Freshly ground black pepper

This comes from John Horne, executive chef of Canoe Restaurant + Bar in Toronto (oliverbonacini.com). He serves it on a square, white platter with artful dollops of cedar jelly, dandelion purée, pickles made with foraged vegetables, Allegretto (a Quebec sheep's milk cheese), and granola. "Bison works really well for carpaccio because it's lean and has a slight game taste to it, which comes through even when sliced thinly but isn't overpowering," says the chef.

Canoe's Bison Tenderloin Carpaccio

Makes 12 servings

To make the cure, in a food processor, combine the salt, brown sugar, thyme, bay leaf, ginger, juniper berries, Sichuan peppercorns, and nutmeg. Blend until evenly mixed. Don't worry about the chunks of berries and peppercorns.

In a shallow dish that can hold the tenderloin, spread a ½-inch layer of the cure. Lay the tenderloin on top of the cure. Pour the remaining cure over the tenderloin. Push the cure all the way around the meat so that it is completely covered. Refrigerate for at least 4 hours, or up to 24 hours. Remove the meat from the cure and brush off any cure sticking to the loin. Discard the cure.

In a medium skillet over high heat, sear the bison in the oil, about 4 minutes. Use tongs to flip the meat, ensuring that all sides are evenly browned.

Cut a large piece of plastic wrap. Roll the tenderloin tightly in the plastic to make a cylinder. Place in the freezer for 1 hour, until the tenderloin sets and you can slice thinly. (Or freeze until ready to use.)

Slice as thinly as possible with a long, sharp knife. If your slices come out too thick, place them between wax paper or plastic wrap and pound with a frying pan or meat mallet to flatten.

To serve, spread the carpaccio out on a platter. If desired, top with greens that have been drizzled with olive oil.

1 cup coarse salt (such as used for canning and pickling)

1½ cups lightly packed dark brown sugar

¼ bunch fresh thyme

1 bay leaf

1½ tsp ground ginger

1½ tsp dried juniper berries

1½ tsp Sichuan peppercorns

½ tsp ground nutmeg

1 lb portion bison tenderloin, fat and silver skin discarded

1 Tbsp sunflower or vegetable oil, for searing

OPTIONAL ACCOMPANIMENTS:
Fresh greens
Extra-virgin olive oil

" We use bison a fair bit as it's a nice change from beef but approachable for people who don't like the taste of game meat. Because of this, guests respond very well to bison. Those guests looking for a less fatty option like bison because it's leaner than beef." —John Horne

Ottawa chef Louis Charest cooks "world-class Canadian cuisine" at Rideau Hall for Governor General David Johnston (and before him, Adrienne Clarkson). He calls this dish Red Salted Canadian Bison Tartare. Red salt refers to the Abkhazian preparation ajika or muhammara, a red chili pepper paste that has many variations throughout the Middle East to Russia. To doll this up even more, add a poached egg on a bed of arugula, drizzled with fresh lemon juice.

Bison Tartare with Muhammara

Makes 6 servings

Just before serving, finely chop the bison by hand. Transfer it to a medium mixing bowl. Add the mustard, shallot, muhammara, capers, and harissa. Mix well. Transfer to a serving dish. Drizzle with oil.

Serve the tartare with the flatbread.

1 lb portion bison tenderloin

1 Tbsp Dijon mustard

2 Tbsp chopped shallot

3 Tbsp purchased or homemade muhammara (see opposite page)

2 Tbsp capers

1 Tbsp purchased or homemade harissa (see opposite page)

Fruity extra-virgin olive oil

1 loaf Middle Eastern flatbread, sliced and toasted

"It's a lean meat. It's a healthy meat. It's a beautiful meat. People who've never had it, once they've tried it, they can't believe how tender it is." —Louis Charest

Chef Louis Charest provides his recipe for muhammara for those who can't find it in a Middle Eastern grocery store. Muhammara, made from red peppers and walnuts, is one of my favorite dips. I use roasted red peppers from a jar, but you can always roast your own.

Muhammara (Spicy Red Pepper + Walnut Dip)

Makes about 1½ cups

In a food processor, combine the bell peppers, walnut pieces, garlic, oil, bread crumbs, pomegranate molasses, tomato paste, cumin, chili flakes, and salt. Process into a chunky dip. Refrigerate, covered, for up to 5 days.

2 roasted red bell peppers (from a jar)
1 cup walnut pieces
1 clove garlic, smashed
¼ cup extra-virgin olive oil
¼ cup dried bread crumbs
2 Tbsp pomegranate molasses
1 Tbsp tomato paste
1 tsp ground cumin
1 tsp red chili flakes
½ tsp fine sea salt

Harissa is a Tunisian/North African hot chili paste that's sold in small cans or jars in North America. Look for it in Middle Eastern grocery stores or fine food stores. It's also simple to make and chef Louis Charest offers this recipe.

Harissa (Hot Chili Paste)

Makes about ¼ cup

Place the chili peppers in a small bowl. Cover with boiling water. Let stand for 15 minutes. Discard the soaking liquid and any stems, but keep the seeds.

In a food processor, combine the chilies, garlic, oil, coriander, caraway, cumin, and salt. Grind into a coarse paste. Refrigerate, covered, for up to 3 weeks.

12 dried red chilies (each about 3 inches long)
3 cloves garlic, minced
2 Tbsp extra-virgin olive oil
1 tsp ground coriander
1 tsp ground caraway
½ tsp ground cumin
½ tsp kosher salt

I have a soft spot for Debu Saha, an Indian chef from Toronto who now works in Quebec City. I first met him when he ran an ambitious but tiny takeout shop, and watched him move on to full-size restaurants. He created this wonderful recipe for me. *Achari* means pickle, and this dish gets an intense, unusual undertone from mixed Indian pickle.

Bison Achari Kebabs with Indian Cucumber + Tomato Salad

Makes 4 servings

In a medium mixing bowl, combine the bison, pickle, yogurt, ginger paste, garlic paste, fresh garlic, chili powder, coriander, cumin, black pepper, onion seeds, oil, and maple syrup. Mix well by hand. Refrigerate, covered, for 6 hours to overnight.

Thread the meat onto 4 short skewers. (Debu uses metal skewers, but if you use wooden ones, soak them for at least 1 hour in water.) Barbecue directly over high heat on an uncovered oiled grill until lightly charred on the outside and still rare to medium-rare inside, about 2 minutes per side. Alternately, cook in a lightly oiled nonstick grill pan over medium-high heat for the same length of time.

Serve the kebabs alongside the salad, if desired.

1 lb portion bison tenderloin (or other tender, boneless steak), cut into 1-inch cubes

2 Tbsp finely chopped mixed Indian pickle (from a jar)

2 Tbsp plain yogurt

1 Tbsp ginger paste

1 Tbsp garlic paste (from a jar)

1½ tsp minced fresh garlic

1½ tsp pure chili powder

1½ tsp ground coriander

1½ tsp ground cumin

1½ tsp freshly ground black pepper

½ tsp black onion seeds

2 Tbsp canola oil

1 Tbsp pure maple syrup

Indian Cucumber + Tomato Salad (optional, see p. 110)

Quebec City chef Debu Saha pairs this Indian-spiced salad with his bison achari kebabs. Chaat masala is a sweet-and-sour spice mix used in Indian and Pakistani cooking that usually includes mango powder, black salt, cumin, coriander, mint, ginger, and pomegranate.

Indian Cucumber + Tomato Salad

Makes about ¼ cup

In a medium mixing bowl, combine the tomatoes, onion, cucumber, mint, cilantro, lemon juice, chaat masala, and cumin. Toss well.

2 tomatoes, chopped

1 small red onion, chopped

1 medium field cucumber, peeled, seeded, and chopped

8 mint leaves, chopped

Handful cilantro leaves, chopped

Juice of 1 lemon

1 tsp chaat masala spice mix

1 tsp cumin seeds, roasted and ground

I've adapted this recipe from thebisoncouncil.com with compliments of Ellie Krieger, a registered dietitian. She hosts *Healthy Appetite* on the Food Network and Cooking Channel, and has written multiple cookbooks. I love how easy this dish is, and how it uses up those jars of artichoke hearts I always seem to have lurking in my cupboard.

Bison Antipasto Skewers with Pesto Dipping Sauce

Makes 24 skewers (for 8 appetizer or 4 main-course servings)

In a medium bowl, whisk together the oil and red wine vinegar. Stir in the garlic.

Add the meat, tossing to coat. Let stand for up to 30 minutes at room temperature or up to 4 hours in the refrigerator. Remove the meat and discard any marinade.

Soak the skewers in hot water for 10 minutes. Drain.

Place 1 piece of artichoke about 2 inches from the point of each skewer. Then, to the pointy end of each skewer, add 1 tomato, and then 1 piece of meat. (If desired, you can refrigerate the prepared skewers in an airtight container for up to 1 day.) When you're ready to cook, lightly sprinkle the meat with salt and pepper to taste.

Cover a barbecue or a large nonstick grill pan with cooking spray. Preheat to medium-high. For the barbecue, place the skewers on the grill and cook for 3 to 4 minutes for medium-rare, turning once. For the grill pan, cook 8 skewers at a time for 3 to 4 minutes for medium-rare, turning once.

To serve, arrange the skewers on a platter with a bowl of pesto for dipping.

2 Tbsp extra-virgin olive oil

1 Tbsp red wine vinegar

1 clove garlic, minced

12 oz bison steak (such as tenderloin, sirloin, or top sirloin), trimmed and cut into 24 small cubes (each about ¾ inch to 1 inch)

24 short (about 6 inches) bamboo skewers

24 pieces drained marinated artichoke hearts

24 grape tomatoes

Kosher salt

Freshly ground black pepper

Cooking spray

½ cup prepared basil pesto

The Heartland Café (heartlandcafe.ca) is housed in an old church in Okotoks, Alberta. Bison sometimes shows up in the daily soup or the popular bacon-wrapped, mushroom-stuffed meatloaf. Borscht is a Ukrainian soup that revolves around beets. This soup doesn't cook for long, so use a tender steak.

Heartland Café's Bison Borscht

Makes about 12 cups (for 6 large servings)

Preheat the oven to 400°F.

Wrap the beets in foil and bake until fork-tender, about 45 to 60 minutes. When cool enough to handle, trim the ends and slip the peels off by hand or with a paring knife. Cut into a ½-inch dice.

In a large nonstick skillet over medium-high, heat 1 tablespoon of the oil. Add the bison. Season with the salt and pepper. Cook until browned on all sides. Transfer to a plate.

In a large pot over medium, heat the remaining 2 tablespoons of oil. Add the onion, celery, and carrots. Cook, stirring, for 7 minutes to soften. Add the cabbage and garlic. Cook, stirring, for 2 minutes. Add the stock, water, bison with any accumulated juices, beets, potatoes, diced tomatoes with their juices, crushed or puréed tomatoes, red wine vinegar, brown sugar, thyme, dill, basil, and paprika. Raise the heat to high and bring to a boil. Reduce the heat to medium and simmer until the vegetables are tender, about 30 minutes to 1 hour. Stir in the parsley.

Serve the soup topped with dollops of sour cream.

5 medium beets, scrubbed
3 Tbsp extra-virgin olive oil, divided
1 lb boneless bison steak, cut into 1-inch chunks and patted dry
1 tsp kosher salt
1 tsp cracked black pepper
1 large yellow onion, cut into ½-inch dice
2 stalks celery, cut into ½-inch dice
2 carrots, peeled and cut into ½-inch dice
2 cups chopped green cabbage
3 cloves garlic, minced
4 cups bison or beef stock
2 cups water
2 Yukon Gold or yellow-fleshed potatoes, peeled, if desired, and cut into ½-inch dice
1 (14 oz) can diced tomatoes
1 cup canned crushed tomatoes or puréed fresh tomatoes
2 Tbsp red wine vinegar
2 Tbsp light brown sugar
2 tsp dried thyme
2 tsp dried dill
2 tsp dried basil
1 tsp paprika
½ cup chopped flat-leaf parsley
Sour cream

When I lived in Hong Kong in the 1990s, I developed a passion for hot pot. It's really just a DIY soup. In a restaurant, you have a pot of bubbling broth on the table and a plate of meat, seafood, and vegetables that you cook yourself. Various sauces are stirred into the broth for a fully personalized meal. It's easy to make hot pot at home. If you have trouble slicing your bison, try freezing it for 30 minutes to 1 hour first.

Bison Hot Pot

Makes 4 servings

For the stock, in a large saucepan, combine the stock, ginger, garlic, shallot, and green onions. Bring to a boil over high heat, and then reduce the heat to low and cover. Simmer 30 minutes. Stir in the rice wine and cilantro. Keep simmering until ready to use.

For the hot pot, cook the vermicelli in a large pot of boiling water according to the package instructions. Drain, and then add to the simmering stock along with the greens and bison. Raise the heat to high and cook just until the greens wilt, about 2 minutes.

For the sauce, in a small bowl, whisk the soy sauce, sesame sauce or tahini, rice wine, and chili-garlic sauce. Stir into the hot pot.

STOCK:
8 cups bison or beef stock
6 thin slices fresh ginger
3 large cloves garlic, minced
1 large shallot, minced
5 green onions, thinly sliced
2 Tbsp Shaoxing rice cooking wine
1 cup chopped cilantro

HOT POT:
1 lb dried rice vermicelli
1 lb Chinese greens, such as quartered baby bok choy and/or shredded napa cabbage
1 lb boneless bison steak, very thinly sliced

SAUCE:
⅓ cup light soy sauce
2 Tbsp Chinese sesame sauce or tahini
1 Tbsp Shaoxing rice cooking wine
1 tsp Asian chili-garlic sauce

North Americans adore the flavors of Thailand and can find ingredients to make the dishes (including curry pastes and dried noodles) in most supermarkets. Once I've opened a jar of curry paste, I work hard to use it up. This bison noodle soup is my chicken noodle soup—and you don't need to be under the weather to enjoy it.

Thai Curry Bison + Rice Noodle Soup

Makes 2 large or 4 small servings

Place the noodles in a large bowl. Cover with boiling water. Let stand for 20 minutes to soften. Drain just before using.

Meanwhile, in a large wok or medium saucepan over medium-high, heat the oil. Add the shallots, garlic, and ginger. Cook, stirring, until softened and fragrant, 3 to 5 minutes. Add the curry paste and stir-fry for 1 minute. Add the bison and stir-fry for 1 minute. Add the stock and bring to a boil over high heat. Add the drained noodles, soy sauce, and fish sauce, if using. Cook for 3 minutes or until the noodles are cooked through. Remove from the heat and stir in the lime leaves, Thai basil, or cilantro.

4 oz Thai dried rice noodles/sticks (any thickness)

2 Tbsp canola oil

2 large shallots, minced

4 large cloves garlic, minced

1 Tbsp peeled and minced ginger

2 to 3 Tbsp Thai red or green curry paste

8 oz bison steak (such as top sirloin), sliced into thin, bite-size pieces

4 cups bison, beef, or vegetable stock

2 Tbsp dark soy sauce

1 Tbsp Asian fish sauce (optional)

4 fresh or dried lime leaves, or ¼ cup slivered fresh Thai basil or chopped cilantro

This bare-bones rendition of a Thai curry delivers maximum flavor with minimal effort. I use Thai Kitchen brand red or green curry paste. They combine red or green chilies with garlic, lemongrass, galangal, salt, onion, lime, coriander, and pepper, and is free of the fermented shrimp paste that comes in some Asian brands.

Thai Curry Bison + Vegetables

Makes 4 servings

In a large saucepan, combine the coconut milk and curry paste. Cook, whisking occasionally, over medium heat for 5 minutes. Stir in the sugar and fish sauce, if using. Add the bison. Raise the heat to medium-high and cook for 5 minutes. Add the vegetables and greens and the lime leaves or Thai basil, if using. Cover and cook for 5 minutes or until the vegetables are crisp-tender and the meat is just cooked.

Serve the curry overtop of, or alongside, bowls of jasmine rice.

2 (14 oz) cans coconut milk

3 Tbsp Thai red or green curry paste, or to taste

2 Tbsp granulated sugar

1 to 2 Tbsp Asian fish sauce (optional)

1 lb bison steak, thinly sliced, then chopped

4 cups mixed bite-size vegetables (such as broccoli florets, green beans, snow peas, red bell pepper) and Asian greens (such as halved baby bok choy, shredded napa cabbage)

4 fresh or dried lime leaves, or ¼ cup slivered fresh Thai basil (optional)

Cooked jasmine rice, for serving

Crispy outside and soft inside, these croquettes from Toronto food writer Monique Savin (twitter.com/moniquesavin) make brilliant use of leftovers. Monique's dip was inspired by Ontario chef Jonathan Gushue's four-cheese mac and cheese with a side of fancy molasses from Nova Scotia. Adding ginger brightens the meat and spuds.

Bison + Parmesan Mash Croquettes with Ginger-Molasses Dip

Makes about 12 croquettes

For the ginger-molasses dip, pour the molasses into a serving bowl. Coarsely grate the ginger on the large holes of a box grater. Bundle the gratings into a piece of cheesecloth and squeeze out the liquid. You need 1 tablespoon of ginger juice for this recipe. Stir the juice into the molasses.

For the Parmesan mash, place the potatoes in a medium saucepan. Cover with water. Bring to a boil over high heat. Cook until fork-tender, about 15 to 30 minutes depending on the size of the potato chunks. Drain. Cover the pan with a kitchen towel. Let stand for 3 minutes. Mash until smooth and glossy using a fork, potato masher, or electric hand-mixer, adding the oil and then the cheese as you mash. Refrigerate until cold. (Makes about 1½ cups.)

For the croquettes, stir the cold bison into the cold mashed potatoes. Using a scant ¼-cup measure, scoop the mixture and shape into 3-inch-long ovals. You should have about 12.

Put the eggs in a shallow bowl. Put the panko or regular bread crumbs into a second shallow bowl. Dip the croquettes in the eggs, letting the excess drip off. Roll the croquettes in the crumbs, coating evenly. If time allows, refrigerate, covered, for at least 30 minutes to firm up.

In a medium nonstick skillet, add a ½ inch of oil. Heat over medium. Add the croquettes, in 2 or 3 batches. Cook, turning with tongs, until golden brown, about 2 to 3 minutes. Drain on a wire rack set over paper towels.

Serve the croquettes with the ginger-molasses dip.

GINGER-MOLASSES DIP:

½ cup fancy molasses

1-inch piece fresh ginger, peeled

PARMESAN MASH:

1 lb russet potatoes, peeled and halved or quartered

2 Tbsp extra-virgin olive oil

½ cup finely grated Parmesan cheese

CROQUETTES:

1½ cups cold cooked and shredded bison steak or roast

2 large eggs, beaten

1 cup panko (Japanese bread crumbs) or unseasoned dried bread crumbs

Canola oil, for frying

This is a favorite of Peter and Judy Haase's at Buffalo Horn Ranch (buffalohornranch.ca) near Eagle Hill, Alberta. Peter was born and raised in Alberta, but his parents were farmers from Germany. He advocates environmentally responsible and sustainable agriculture.

Buffalo Horn Ranch's Bison Stroganoff

Makes 4 servings

Slice the bison into thin strips, about 2 inches long by ½ inch wide. Spread the meat out on a platter. Sprinkle with the pepper. Cover with the onion. Let stand, loosely covered with wax paper or plastic wrap, at room temperature for 1 hour.

In a small saucepan over medium heat, melt 2 tablespoons of the butter. Stir in the flour. Cook, stirring, for 1 minute. Whisk in the stock. Cook, stirring, until thickened, about 3 to 5 minutes. Stir in the mustard and salt to taste. Remove from the heat.

In a large sauté pan or skillet over medium-high, melt the remaining 2 tablespoons of butter. Add the bison, onion, and mushrooms. Cook, stirring, until browned, about 7 to 8 minutes. Add the sauce. Reduce the heat to low. Simmer, uncovered, for 10 to 15 minutes, stirring occasionally. Remove from the heat. Stir in the sour cream.

Meanwhile, in large saucepan of boiling, salted water, cook the egg noodles as per package instructions; drain.

Serve the bison stroganoff over the noodles.

1 lb boneless bison steak (such as top sirloin, sirloin tip, round steak, or stir-fry strips)

½ tsp freshly ground black pepper

1 medium yellow onion, halved and thinly sliced

4 Tbsp unsalted butter, divided

2 Tbsp all-purpose flour

1 cup bison or beef stock

1 tsp Dijon mustard

Kosher salt

1 cup sliced white button or cremini mushrooms

¼ cup sour cream

12 oz dried broad egg noodles

Canadian Rocky Mountain Resorts (crmr.com) owns a clutch of resorts and restaurants, as well as the Canadian Rocky Mountain Ranch, where it raises bison and elk. This hash is served in various incarnations at all of its lodges. This version is served with poached eggs, but if it's easier to fry your eggs (like we did in the picture), go ahead.

Canadian Rocky Mountain Resorts' Bison Hash

Makes 4 servings

Bring a large pot of water to boil over high heat. Add the potatoes. Cook for 2 minutes. Drain well.

Sprinkle the bison with salt and pepper.

In a large nonstick skillet over medium-high, heat the oil. Add the bison. Cook, stirring until browned, about 2 minutes. Add the potatoes, corn, red onion, and red pepper. Cook, stirring, for 5 minutes to soften. Add the stock, tomatoes, and 1 tablespoon of herbs. Bring to a boil. Cook until the liquid is reduced by half, about 2 minutes. Stir in the butter.

Meanwhile, to poach the eggs, bring a large shallow saucepan of water to a gentle boil over medium-high heat. Reduce the heat to a gentle simmer. Add the vinegar. Crack the eggs, one by one, into a small cup or bowl. Gently slip each egg into the water. Cover the pan and cook the eggs for 3 minutes, so the egg whites are cooked but the yolks are still runny. Remove the eggs immediately with a slotted spoon. Pat dry with paper towels.

To serve, divide the hash among 4 plates. Place 1 poached egg on top of each serving. Sprinkle the plates with the remaining 1 tablespoon of herbs.

4 medium Yukon Gold potatoes, peeled and cut into ½-inch dice

1 cup boneless bison steak, cut into thin strips or ½-inch cubes

Kosher salt

Freshly ground black pepper

2 Tbsp canola oil

½ cup corn

½ cup diced red onion

¼ cup diced red bell pepper

½ cup bison or beef stock

¼ cup halved cherry or grape tomatoes

2 Tbsp chopped fresh herbs (such as thyme, rosemary, chives, parsley, cilantro), divided

2 Tbsp unsalted butter

2 tsp white vinegar

4 large eggs

" It's just nice that we know where our animals are raised. Dr. Terry Church is our ranch manager, and I can email him or call him. He doesn't tell me the names of the bison I have in the kitchen, but he probably could." —Thomas Neukom, head chef at the Lake House (formerly the Ranche), Calgary, Alberta

The Hunt

I'm transfixed as buffalo after buffalo tumbles to its death over a sandstone cliff in the foothills of the Rocky Mountains. The majestic beasts have been outwitted by the Blackfoot people in an ingenious communal hunt that will provide food, clothing, shelter, tools, and weapons.

The Plains Indians know the land and they understand the buffalo. They patiently guide the herd from a grazing area in the Porcupine Hills to "V-shaped drive lanes" they've created with rock clusters and tree branches. One hunter imitates a lost calf. The others, dressed in buffalo or coyote robes, spook the herd into a mass stampede so the buffalo gallop over the cliff and plummet 33 feet (10 meters) to their deaths. At the bottom of the cliff, tribe members finish off any wounded animals, gut the carcasses, and drag them to a nearby butchering camp where every part of the animal will be eaten or used. Horns are formed into spoons. Marrow bones are a treat. Some meat is sun-dried, pulverized, and mixed with buffalo fat and berries to make pemmican, which will keep for months.

The movie ends. The lights come up in the theater at Head-Smashed-In Buffalo Jump. We've just watched *Piskun the Buffalo Jump*, a docudrama about the way buffalo were hunted right here, where this building now stands, for nearly 6,000 years.

I'm at the jump with the Bison Producers of Alberta (bisoncentre.com) for a tour, history lesson, and lunch before we have a private association meeting.

We learn that "head-smashed-in" doesn't refer to a buffalo. The name comes from the true story of a Peigan boy whose head was crushed when he got caught in the crush of corpses while watching the hunt from the bottom of the cliff.

TERRY KREMENIUK, EXECUTIVE DIRECTOR OF THE CANADIAN BISON ASSOCIATION, AT THE HEAD-SMASHED-IN BUFFALO JUMP, 2013

Don't worry, our guide reassures us—no animals were killed in the making of this film. The dead buffalo came from a processing plant; the live ones came from local herds.

There's one particular buffalo in the film that seems to enjoy his close-ups and radiates calm. "It was our buffalo, Bailey, that they used in this film," says Linda Sautner, the office manager for the Bison Producers, bursting with pride. She and her husband, Jim, gained fame for raising Bailey D. Buffalo as a pet. He starred in several films before his untimely, accidental death. The Sautners are now raising a second pet buffalo named Bailey Jr.

This place, a 1,470-acre (595-hectare) archaeological site, is considered one of the oldest, largest, and best-preserved buffalo jumps in North America. In 1981, it was declared a UNESCO World Heritage Site, on par with the Egyptian pyramids, Stonehenge, and the Galápagos Islands. The multilevel interpretative center, nestled discreetly in the Porcupine Hills near Fort Macleod, Alberta, opened in 1987. Millions of people have visited the site.

Our Blackfoot guide, Stan, walks us to the top level so we can go outside to the edge of one of the jumps. "That climb was 137 steps," he says at one point. "It only represents one third of the drop, so it kind of gives you an idea of how lethal the drop was."

We stand outside in the hot summer sun imagining what once went on here, long before guns came along and changed the hunt.

Back inside the interpretive center, there's a fiberglass replica of one of the cliffs with three buffalo poised to tumble over the edge. A three-member herd doesn't capture the drama of the mass hunt, and the display is badly faded.

Peter Haase, one of the ranchers with our group, reveals that five of his bison have been preserved through taxidermy and will help revamp this key display. He and his wife, Judy, who run Buffalo Horn Ranch near Calgary, met the government's three rules to be part of the project. Their herd is registered pure plains bison. Their animals weren't

slaughtered just for the display. And the animals mainly look female—a requirement based on the fact that archaeological records show very few bull bones were found at the site. (It wasn't breeding season when the herds were usually run off the cliffs, so the bulls hadn't joined the herds.)

There will be a 15-year-old cow that couldn't get pregnant, a pair of two-year-old heifers raised for meat, and a calf that died a few days after birth. The cow and heifers are in running and jumping positions, but only the calf's hide will be used.

The fifth animal is Hector, an eight-year-old breeding bull who needed to be culled because he was becoming too closely related to the herd. He will be used in a static display in a standing position.

The Haases consider it "something of an honor" to be part of the Head-Smashed-In display. For 20 years, they have made it part of their mission to help conserve the plains bison as a pure species while other ranchers cross plains and wood bison for a bigger, faster animal. "The display will create a lasting legacy for our herd," says Peter.

I can't wait to see it. But today's most compelling display is a suspended bison skeleton. It clearly shows the unusual bone structure of the hump, something I've been wanting my butcher to include in an eye-catching pot roast (more on that in the next story). Suddenly my haphazard bone garden back at the ranch seems amateur. Next time one of our bison dies in the field, I'm going to gather all of the bones and try to replicate this display myself.

CHAPTER 4

Roasts

Just like steaks, premium bison roasts should be cooked to rare, medium-rare, or medium. But I undercook them by 10°F because the temperature will rise while the meat rests, which I recommend doing for 20 minutes. I veer closer to the temperatures used by chefs for cooking roasts. For pot roasts, cook until they're fork-tender.

- Rare is 135°F so cook to 125°F.
- Medium-rare is 145°F so cook to 135°F.
- Medium 155°F so cook to 145°F.

Use a digital thermometer with a stainless steel probe and timer so you can keep tabs on your roasts without opening the oven. Otherwise, be sure your thermometer is ovenproof. Always insert the probe in the thickest part of the roast, ensuring that it doesn't touch any bones.

Tender roasts (like rib, striploin, tenderloin, and sirloin)
Let the tender roast stand at room temperature for 1 hour before cooking. Cook the roast uncovered on a roasting rack in an oven heated to 275°F. Use a digital thermometer. I hate to say anything negative about bison, but because there is minimal fat and marbling, you may not get many pan drippings to make gravy. There, I've admitted it.

Medium tender roasts (like sirloin tip, eye of round, inside round, and outside round)
Season the roast, rub it with oil, and sear it in a skillet over medium-high. Then, cook the roast in a covered roasting pan with ¼ cup of water or wine at 275°F. Use a digital thermometer.

Less tender roasts (like blade roasts, cross-rib, and brisket)
"Pot roast" should be seasoned, rubbed with oil, and seared in a skillet over medium-high. You don't need a thermometer. Cook the roast in a covered pan with liquid (anything goes: wine, beer, soda pop, canned tomatoes, water, juice) at 300°F. Cook low and slow until the meat can be easily pulled apart with a fork. The roast tastes best when made one day and eaten the next. Reheat the roast in its liquid in the oven or on the stove.

Air North, the Yukon's airline, is proud of its food. Chef Michael Bock designed the menu and loves using local products like bison. This roast is seasoned with a powerful rub that has the unusual addition of cardamom. This rub can be used on any steak as well. The dish doesn't really need the cranberry relish, but the relish is so good I had to include it.

Air North's Coffee + Cardamom Bison with Cranberry Relish

Makes 6 to 8 servings

For the rub, in a small bowl, combine the coffee, salt, brown sugar, paprika, cardamom, ginger, garlic, and olive oil. Mix well into a thick paste. Rub all over the bison. Wrap the roast in plastic and let it stand at room temperature for 30 minutes to 1 hour.

Preheat the oven to 275°F.

In a medium cast-iron or heavy ovenproof skillet over medium-high, heat the canola oil. Add the roast. Cook for 2 minutes per side, flipping with tongs. Insert an ovenproof digital thermometer in the thickest part of the meat.

Transfer the skillet to the oven. Cook to 125°F for rare, 135°F for medium-rare, or 145°F for medium. Transfer the roast to a cutting board. Let stand, loosely covered with foil, for 20 minutes before slicing. The temperature will rise.

Serve the bison with the cranberry relish, if desired.

2 Tbsp freshly ground medium roast coffee

2 Tbsp coarse sea salt

2 Tbsp dark brown sugar

1 Tbsp paprika

1½ tsp ground cardamom

1½ tsp ground ginger

1 Tbsp minced garlic

2 Tbsp extra-virgin olive oil

2 lb portion bison tenderloin or boneless striploin, patted dry

1 Tbsp canola oil

Air North's Cranberry Relish (optional, see opposite page)

There's a lot going on in this knockout relish, created by Air North chef Michael Bock. He pairs it with his coffee- and cardamom-rubbed bison, but I'm sure you'll find plenty of ways to enjoy it.

Air North's Cranberry Relish

Makes about 2 cups

In a medium saucepan over medium-high heat, combine the orange juice, raspberry balsamic vinegar, sugar, honey, onion, and garlic. Bring to a simmer. Add the bell pepper, ginger, cloves, coriander, and chili flakes. Simmer for 5 minutes. Add the cranberries. Bring to a slow boil, and gently cook for 10 minutes or until the berries begin to pop, stirring occasionally with a wooden spoon. Let cool. Remove the cloves before serving.

Refrigerate, covered, for up to 3 weeks.

¼ cup orange juice

¼ cup raspberry balsamic vinegar

¾ cup granulated sugar

¼ cup honey

½ cup finely chopped Spanish onion or other sweet onion

3 cloves garlic, minced

½ cup finely chopped yellow or green bell pepper

1½ tsp peeled and minced ginger

3 whole cloves

1½ tsp coriander seeds, roasted and coarsely crushed

¼ tsp red chili flakes

2 cups fresh or frozen cranberries

Spanish smoked paprika is another must-have in my kitchen arsenal because my husband adores strong flavors.

Bison Tenderloin Rubbed with Smoked Paprika + Cumin

Makes 6 to 8 servings

Let the meat stand at room temperature for 30 minutes to 1 hour. Pat dry with paper towels.

In a mortar using a pestle, grind the garlic and salt into paste. Stir in the smoked paprika, cumin, pepper, and oil. Rub all over the tenderloin.

Preheat the oven to 275°F.

Heat a medium cast-iron or ovenproof skillet over medium-high for at least 15 minutes. Add the tenderloin. Sear all over, turning with tongs, about 2 minutes per side. Insert an ovenproof digital thermometer in the thickest part of the meat.

Transfer the skillet to the oven. Cook to 125°F for rare, 135°F for medium-rare, or 145°F for medium. Transfer the roast to a cutting board. Let stand, loosely covered with foil, for 20 minutes before slicing. The temperature will rise.

2 lb portion bison tenderloin

3 cloves garlic, peeled

1 tsp kosher salt

2 tsp smoked paprika

1 tsp ground cumin

1 tsp freshly ground black pepper

1 Tbsp extra-virgin olive oil

RIGHT: HAZEL MACKENZIE

Dave Carter, executive director of the National Bison Association (bisoncentral.com), created this assertive rub. The gorgeous black crust with intense flavor plays off of the sweet, tender meat. You can use this rub with any size roast. As for the unusual method of leaving the roast to sit in a hot oven that has been turned all the way down, Dave "swiped that technique years ago" from the Junior League. "Cooking it nice and slow allows that meat to tenderize," he says. "I just think this is the best way to cook a roast."

Dave Carter's Coffee + Black Pepper–Rubbed Bison Rib Roast

Makes about 12 servings

Let the roast stand at room temperature for 30 minutes to 1 hour. Pat dry with paper towels. Using a sharp knife, score any fat.

Preheat the oven to 400°F.

Place the coffee beans and peppercorns in a spice grinder or coffee grinder. Pulse until coarsely crushed. Transfer to a bowl. Stir in the garlic.

Rub the roast with oil, and then coat all over with the coffee-pepper rub.

Place the roast, rib side down, on a rack in a roasting pan. Insert an ovenproof digital thermometer in the thickest part of the roast without touching any bone. Loosely cover the roast with foil. Roast in the oven for 30 minutes. Turn the oven temperature down to 325°F, and cook until the thermometer registers 125°F for rare, 135°F for medium-rare, or 145°F for medium. Alternately, after roasting for 30 minutes, turn the oven to the lowest setting (usually 170°F) without opening the door. You can leave the roast for up to 4 hours like this. About 1 hour before serving, turn the oven to 325°F and finish cooking.

Transfer the roast to a cutting board. Cover loosely with foil. Let stand for 20 minutes, so the temperature will rise, before slicing as desired.

About 4 lb bison standing rib roast or bone-in prime rib roast

¼ cup arabica dark roast coffee beans

¼ cup black peppercorns

4 cloves garlic, minced

Extra-virgin olive oil

Prime rib is a glorious (and expensive) cut of meat that deserves respect and gentle treatment. Here I've simply rubbed the meat with fresh herbs, garlic, and oil (feel free to use whatever herbs you have on hand). Since bison doesn't often have enough pan drippings to make gravy, I've added an optional onion gravy.

Herbaceous Bison Prime Rib with Onion Gravy

Makes about 12 servings

Let the roast stand at room temperature for 30 minutes to 1 hour. Pat dry with paper towels. Using a sharp knife, score any fat.

Preheat the oven to 450°F.

In a bowl, stir the garlic, thyme, rosemary, salt, and oil into a paste. Rub all over the bison. Insert an ovenproof digital thermometer in the center of the roast without touching any bone.

Place the meat, fat side up, on a rack in a roasting pan. Roast for 20 minutes. Reduce the heat to 275°F. Cook to 125°F for rare, 135°F for medium-rare, or 145°F for medium, at least 2½ hours. Transfer the roast to a cutting board. Let stand, loosely covered, for 20 minutes before slicing. The temperature will rise.

Serve with onion gravy, if desired.

4 lb bison prime rib roast

¼ cup minced garlic

¼ cup finely chopped fresh thyme

¼ cup finely chopped fresh rosemary

1 Tbsp kosher salt

2 Tbsp extra-virgin olive oil

Onion Gravy (optional, see opposite page)

I once went on a road trip to Ithaca, New York, to eat at the famous vegetarian Moosewood Restaurant (moosewoodcooks.com) and have long loved their food. When my oldest daughter, Lucy, was about nine, she became a vegetarian, so I'm always trying to come up with food she likes. This recipe started as a vegetarian gravy from *Moosewood Restaurant Celebrates* (Clarkson Potter, 2003), but has evolved into a bison-stock-based gravy since Lucy (still a vegetarian) doesn't actually like gravy.

Onion Gravy

Makes about 3 cups

In a large skillet over medium-high, heat the oil. Add the onions. Cook, stirring, for 5 minutes. Add the herbs. Cook, stirring often, until the onions are browned and fried, about 45 minutes, reducing the heat as needed. Add the soy sauce and stock. Raise the heat to medium-high and bring the mixture to a boil.

In a small bowl, whisk the cornstarch and cold water until smooth. Stir into the onion mixture in a thin, steady stream. Cook, stirring constantly, for 5 minutes or until thickened. Taste the gravy and season to taste with pepper.

2 Tbsp canola oil

6 cups halved and thinly sliced onions (sweet, white, yellow, or red)

1 Tbsp finely chopped mixed fresh herbs (such as rosemary, thyme, oregano, and marjoram)

3 Tbsp light soy sauce

2 cups bison, beef, or vegetable stock

2 Tbsp cornstarch

¼ cup cold water

Freshly ground black pepper

Just when I think it's silly to keep ordering prime rib in a restaurant (how different can it possibly be?), along comes CHARCUT Roast House (charcut.com). Sure, the Calgary, Alberta, restaurant spit-roasts its meat and I can't duplicate that. But I loved how it presented the meal. The prime rib was topped with some lightly dressed baby arugula. Alongside were half a grilled lemon, a whole bulb of roasted garlic, a tiny tumbler of jus, a small bowl of flaky sea salt, and a small dish of horseradish cream. Perfection.

Bison Prime Rib with All the Fixings

Makes 2 servings

For the roasted garlic, preheat the oven to 400°F. Peel away the outer layers of skin from the heads. Using a sharp knife, cut off the top ½ inch of each head, exposing the tops of the individual cloves. Place the heads on a large piece of foil. Drizzle with oil. Wrap the foil around the heads so they are completely covered. Bake until the heads are soft when squeezed, about 45 to 60 minutes. Keep warm until ready to serve. To eat, use the tines of your fork or your fingers to pull out the cloves.

Meanwhile, for the meat, score any fat. Let the roast stand at room temperature for 30 minutes to 1 hour. Pat dry with paper towels. Mix the salt and pepper, and then rub the mixture all over the meat. Rub the meat with oil.

Preheat the oven to 275°F.

Heat a large cast-iron skillet over medium for at least 15 minutes. Sear the meat for 2 minutes per side. Insert an ovenproof digital thermometer in the center of the meat without touching the bone.

Transfer the skillet to the oven. Cook to 125°F for rare, 135°F for medium-rare, or 145°F for medium, at least 40 minutes. Transfer the roast to a cutting board. Let stand, loosely covered, for 20 minutes before slicing. The temperature will rise.

Continued on page 136

ROASTED GARLIC:
2 heads garlic
Extra-virgin olive oil

PRIME RIB + GRAVY:
1-bone bison prime rib roast (about 1½ lb)
1 Tbsp kosher salt
2 tsp freshly ground black pepper
Extra-virgin olive oil
2 Tbsp all-purpose flour
2 cups bison or beef stock

GRILLED LEMON:
1 lemon, halved
Canola oil

HORSERADISH-CREAM SAUCE:
½ cup sour cream
2 Tbsp drained prepared hot horseradish
Freshly ground black pepper

FOR SERVING:
2 cups baby arugula
1 Tbsp extra-virgin olive oil
Flaky sea salt (such as Maldon)

Continued from page 134

For the gravy, return the skillet with any pan juices to the stove over medium heat. Add the flour. Cook, whisking, for 1 to 2 minutes. Whisk in the stock. Cook, whisking and scraping up any browned bits from the pan, for 2 minutes. Raise the heat to high. Cook until the liquid reduces and thickens slightly, about 10 minutes. Strain into a gravy boat.

Meanwhile, for the grilled lemon, discard any visible seeds from the lemon halves. Brush the lemon with the oil. Heat a grill pan over medium-high. Place the lemon halves, cut sides down, in the pan. Cook, undisturbed, until lightly charred, 2 to 3 minutes. Serve warm.

For the horseradish-cream sauce, in a small bowl, stir together the sour cream and horseradish. Season to taste with pepper. Stir well.

To serve, in a small bowl, toss the arugula and oil. Slice the roast into 2 generous pieces (only 1 person will get the bone). Place 1 prime rib slice on each of 2 plates. Top each with arugula. Put 1 lemon half and 1 head of garlic on each plate. Pass the gravy, flaky sea salt, and horseradish-cream sauce separately.

This showcase roast usually needs little adornment, but a flavorful Cajun rub does complement things. I am partial to the President's Choice Cajun seasoning grinder. It blends sea salt, paprika, garlic, onion, black and white peppercorns, chili pepper, cumin, oregano, thyme, and sage.

Bison Prime Rib with Cajun Rub

Makes about 12 servings

Score any fat on the top of the roast. Let the roast stand at room temperature for 30 minutes to 1 hour.

Preheat the oven to 450°F.

Pat the roast dry with paper towels. Rub all over with the Cajun spice. Insert an ovenproof digital thermometer in the center of the roast without touching any bone.

Place the roast, fat side up, on a rack in a roasting pan. Roast for 20 minutes to brown. Reduce the heat to 275°F, and cook to 125°F for rare, 135°F for medium-rare, or 145°F for medium, at least 2 hours. Transfer the roast to a cutting board and cover loosely with foil. Let it stand for 20 minutes, so the temperature can rise, before slicing.

Serve with onion gravy, if desired.

4 lb bison prime rib roast

⅓ cup Cajun spice blend, or to taste

Onion Gravy (optional, see p. 133)

You'll find this among the recipes and cooking tips at ilovebison.com, the consumer website for the Canadian Bison Association. It's a good way to turn a less popular roast into something special.

Honey Mustard–Crusted Bison Roast

Makes 6 to 8 servings

Let the roast stand at room temperature for 30 minutes to 1 hour. Pat dry with paper towels. In a bowl, combine the salt, ground pepper, and paprika. Rub all over the meat. Rub the meat with oil.

Preheat the oven to 275°F.

Heat a large cast-iron skillet over medium-high for at least 15 minutes. Add the roast. Cook until browned all over, about 8 minutes. Transfer the roast to a rack in a roasting pan. Add the water. Insert an ovenproof digital thermometer in the center of the roast.

In a bowl, stir together the honey mustard, Dijon mustard, garlic, oregano, sage, and cracked pepper. Spread over the top of the roast.

Transfer the skillet to the oven. Cook to 125°F for rare, 135°F for medium-rare, or 145°F for medium. Transfer the roast to a cutting board. Let stand, loosely covered with foil, for 20 minutes before slicing. The temperature will rise.

To serve, thinly slice the meat against the grain.

2 lb bison tri-tip, sirloin tip, or inside round roast

2 tsp kosher salt

1 tsp freshly ground black pepper

1 tsp paprika

Extra-virgin olive oil

1 cup water

½ cup honey mustard

¼ cup Dijon mustard

10 cloves garlic, minced

3 Tbsp chopped fresh oregano

3 Tbsp chopped fresh sage

1 tsp cracked black pepper

Pomegranate juice has exploded onto the grocery scene, giving cranberry juice fierce competition. Don't just drink it—braise with it and enjoy its lovely tartness and depth of flavor. Traditional wisdom says to thinly slice your brisket against the grain, but I like serving it in chunks.

Bison Brisket Braised in Pomegranate Juice

Makes 8 servings

Heat 1 tablespoon of the oil in a large roasting pan over medium-high. Add the brisket. Brown all over, about 5 minutes per side. Transfer the meat to a platter.

Preheat the oven to 300°F.

Add the remaining 1 tablespoon oil to the pan. Add the onions, carrots, celery, and garlic. Cook over medium-high, stirring, for 6 minutes to soften the vegetables. Add the pomegranate juice, thyme, and rosemary. Raise the heat to high and bring to a boil. Add the brisket and any accumulated juices. Cover the pot and transfer it to the oven. Cook until the meat is fork-tender, turning the meat occasionally, about 4 hours.

Alternately, transfer the browned brisket to a slow cooker. Add the onions, carrots, celery, garlic, pomegranate juice, thyme, and rosemary. Cook according to the manufacturer's instructions, on low or high heat as desired, until the meat is fork-tender.

When the meat is cooked, transfer it to a cutting board. Cut as desired, either in thin slices against the grain, or in 8 serving-size pieces.

Strain the braising liquid, discarding the thyme and rosemary sprigs. Using a slotted spoon, transfer the vegetables to a food processor or blender. Add 1 cup of the braising liquid and purée. Combine the puréed mixture and the remaining braising liquid in a medium saucepan. Bring to a boil over high heat and boil until it's reduced to desired consistency for sauce. Transfer to a bowl or measuring cup. Season to taste with salt and pepper. Pass the sauce alongside the brisket.

2 Tbsp canola oil, divided

4 lb portion bison brisket

3 medium yellow onions, chopped

2 large carrots, peeled and chopped

1 stalk celery, chopped

6 large cloves garlic, minced

4 cups pomegranate juice

4 sprigs fresh thyme

2 sprigs fresh rosemary

Kosher salt

Freshly ground black pepper

Chef Talia Syrie runs the Tallest Poppy (thetallestpoppy.com), a locally minded restaurant in Winnipeg, Manitoba. This is the base of a popular pulled bison salad (see opposite page) that she used to make. You can always eat this hot as a main course, or pile it into a sandwich.

The Tallest Poppy's Pulled Bison

Makes about 4 cups of meat or 8 servings

In a bowl, combine the brown sugar, salt, black pepper, cayenne pepper, oregano, paprika, cumin, and coffee. Rub all over the bison. Make 2 small slashes in the roast, and insert the garlic cloves. Place the roast in a slow cooker. Surround with the onions, carrots, and celery. Add the wine and water. Cook, according to the manufacturer's instructions, on high or low as desired, until very tender (about 4 hours on high).

Transfer the meat to a cutting board. Strain the braising liquid, discarding the solids. Put the liquid in a pot on the stove and boil over medium-high until reduced to desired thickness for sauce.

For pulled meat, use two forks to pull the roast into shreds, discarding any fat and keeping any garlic that hasn't fallen out to eat hot. If you prefer, serve the roast in pieces.

Serve the meat with the braising liquid passed separately.

1 Tbsp light brown sugar

1 tsp kosher salt

½ tsp freshly ground black pepper

½ tsp cayenne pepper

½ tsp dried oregano leaves

½ tsp paprika

½ tsp ground cumin

½ tsp ground coffee

2 lb boneless bison roast (such as brisket, blade, or chuck), patted dry

2 cloves garlic, peeled

3 large yellow onions, quartered

2 carrots, peeled and chopped

2 stalks celery, chopped

½ cup red wine

½ cup water

At the Tallest Poppy in Winnipeg, Manitoba (thetallestpoppy.com), chef/owner Talia Syrie created this cold salad as an alternative to the usual hot pulled-meat sandwich.

The Tallest Poppy's Pulled Bison Salad

Makes 2 servings

In a medium bowl, combine the bison, pickles, bell pepper, garlic, mayonnaise, sour cream, and grainy mustard. Season to taste with salt and pepper. Stir well.

Divide the greens over 2 plates. Top each plate with half of the pulled bison. Garnish each plate with tomatoes, red onion, and radishes.

2 cups cold pulled bison (see opposite page)

2 medium dill pickles, finely chopped

½ yellow bell pepper, finely chopped

2 cloves roasted garlic (see Cooking Tip), mashed

3 Tbsp mayonnaise

1 Tbsp sour cream

1 Tbsp grainy Dijon mustard

Kosher salt

Freshly ground black pepper

4 cups mixed salad greens

12 cherry or grape tomatoes, halved if desired

½ red onion, thinly sliced

2 radishes, chopped

Cooking Tip: To roast garlic, preheat the oven to 400°F. Wrap a head of garlic in foil and roast until soft, about 1 hour. Slice off the top of the garlic head and squeeze the flesh out of each clove.

Bison roasts stay gorgeously moist when they're braised, and brawny boneless blade roasts are my favorite. This is one of the first things I cooked at the ranch after I bought a slow cooker. If there's room in your pot, throw in onions, potatoes, or carrots. Serve this pot roast with rice or veggies and salad. Reheat any leftover meat in a saucepan over low heat in its sauce.

Bison Pot Roast with Chipotle-Tomato Sauce

Makes 8 servings

In a food processor or blender, combine the chipotle purée, tomatoes with their juices, and garlic. Purée until smooth.

Generously season the roast with salt and pepper.

Preheat the oven to 300°F.

In a large ovenproof roasting pan over medium-high, heat the oil. Add the roast. Brown all over, turning with tongs, about 8 minutes total. Pour the chipotle-tomato sauce over the meat. Cover and cook in the oven, stirring occasionally and ladling the sauce over the meat, until the meat is fork-tender, about 4 hours.

If using a slow cooker, brown the roast in a skillet. Add the roast to the slow cooker and pour the chipotle-tomato sauce overtop. Cover and cook according to the manufacturer's instructions, on low or high heat as desired, until the meat is fork-tender.

Transfer the roast to a cutting board to slice as desired. Stir the cilantro into the chipotle-tomato sauce. Pass sauce separately in a serving bowl.

3 Tbsp puréed canned chipotle chilies packed in adobo sauce (see Cooking Tip, p. 32)

1 (28 oz) can tomatoes (whole, diced, or stewed)

6 large cloves garlic, minced

4 lb bison pot roast (boneless blade or cross-rib), patted dry

Kosher salt

Freshly ground black pepper

1 Tbsp canola oil

¼ cup chopped cilantro

Desperately Seeking a Hump Roast

I dream of eating a hump roast with long feather bones "arcing spectacularly skyward." It's an image that I drooled over while reading *The Fort Cookbook: New Foods of the Old West from the Famous Denver Restaurant* (HarperCollins, 1997) by Samuel P. Arnold.

The late restaurateur was so transfixed by stories of Native Americans feasting on bison humps that he enlisted Bob Dineen of Rocky Mountain Natural Meats to cut a hump roast. The bison's distinctive shoulder hump helps support the animal's huge head as it plows through snow. It's filled with muscle supported by wide, long "feather bones," but there is supposed to be some tender meat in there somewhere.

Alas, it's an old cookbook—it was published in 1997—and the bison-friendly Fort restaurant no longer serves this kind of bony hump roast, so I reached out to Bob Dineen for advice.

"That was a long time ago, and to tell you the truth it really was not that great," he admits. "Sam Arnold and I cut a whole front quarter up to try and get an actual hump, but the muscle that lies just under the fat is very grainy, fatty, and tough. We ended up just using a chuck roast." It didn't fly for the restaurant, Bob remembers, because the meat had to be slow-roasted and served right away and couldn't be served later in individual portions. He does have one fond memory of dining at the Fort on a pile of carved, roasted hump meat served on "a cradle of bones."

Bob doesn't cut feather-bone hump roasts these days. But he does process more bison than anyone else in North America—more than 500 a week. He handles all of Ted Turner's bison and supplies the Ted's Montana Grill chain as well as Costco and numerous supermarkets. His top-selling product is ground burger meat.

I photocopied the hump page from the Fort cookbook for my Alberta butcher when we did our last slaughter and talked to him about it by phone. He gamely attempted to cut me a photo-worthy hump roast for this cookbook, but ended up giving me three huge untrimmed roasts with the gorgeous bones concealed. When my husband brought two of them to me in Ontario, I hacked away at one but just made a mess of things. The meat was delicious, and I roasted the bones separately, but they just looked silly together. The second roast wound up at the photo shoot and looks quite lovely at the opening of this chapter (page 125).

I haven't given up. Next time I go in for a butchering, I'll show the guys what I want. Until then, my hump dreams are on hold.

Bœuf bourguignon is a French stew made famous by Julia Child, but it can be time-consuming and finicky. Anne Garrido, who is French and who used to be in charge of the bison at Bouvry Exports in Alberta, makes hers this way. "A good wine is going to make a good sauce," she stresses. "If your budget doesn't allow for real Burgundy, use a good pinot noir." She buys her bacon at a farmers' market. Read about Anne in "The Dinner Plates of Paris" (pp. 75–79). Serve this stew with potatoes or broad egg noodles.

Bison Bourguignon

Makes 6 to 8 servings

In a large pot over medium-high heat, cook the bacon until crisp, about 7 to 9 minutes. Transfer to a plate with a slotted spoon. Add the bison to the pot with the bacon fat in a single layer (or in batches if necessary). Sprinkle with the flour. Cook until well browned all over, about 8 minutes. Add the onions and garlic. Cook, stirring, for 5 minutes. Add the carrots, mushrooms, and bouquet garni. Season to taste with salt and pepper. Stir in the wine and bacon.

Bring to a boil over high heat, and then reduce the heat to medium or medium-low and cover. Simmer, stirring occasionally, until the meat is tender, about 3 to 4 hours.

4 thick slices double-smoked bacon, chopped

2 lb bison chuck (such as cross-rib or brisket), cut into 1-inch chunks and patted dry

2 Tbsp all-purpose flour

2 medium yellow onions, chopped

2 cloves garlic, minced

3 carrots, peeled and cut into chunks

8 oz white button mushrooms, trimmed and halved

1 bouquet garni (1 sprig fresh rosemary, 3 sprigs fresh thyme, and 2 bay leaves tied with kitchen twine)

Kosher salt

Freshly ground black pepper

1 (25.4 oz) bottle red Burgundy or pinot noir

"When the colder Canadian months set in, there is nothing better than something braised," says Timothy Wasylko, executive chef of 24 Sussex Drive. "You will notice that I am using a white wine for this recipe. I find it complements the richness of the stewed bison and cooked beans without overpowering the natural flavor of the bison." This "go-to Wasylko family recipe" came from serving leftover bison short ribs with leftover beans from a French cassoulet. To speed things up, use about 2½ cups canned beans. For this photo, we served the stew over a slice of grilled toast. You can do the same, or just serve it in a bowl with bread alongside.

Bison + Bean Stew with Wilted Swiss Chard

Makes 6 servings

In a medium bowl filled with water, soak the beans overnight. Drain. Rinse.

Preheat the oven to 300°F.

In a large ovenproof pot or casserole dish over medium-high, heat 2 tablespoons of the oil until just smoking. Carefully add the bison in a single layer (or in batches if necessary). Cook until browned, about 3 to 4 minutes. Transfer the meat to a plate. Add the remaining 1 tablespoon of oil and the onions and garlic to the pot. Cook, stirring, for 7 minutes. Add the mushrooms and wine. Raise the heat to high. Boil for 3 minutes. Return the bison and its juices to the pot. Add the tomatoes with their juices plus the beans, stock, thyme, salt, and pepper.

Cover the pot and transfer to the oven. Cook, stirring occasionally, until the bison and beans are tender, about 2 to 2½ hours. Stir in the chard and cover. Let the dish stand for 5 minutes before serving.

"Bison is definitely a go-to meat if I have visitors come from other countries." —Timothy Wasylko

½ cup dried white navy beans, rinsed

½ cup dried red kidney beans, rinsed

3 Tbsp canola oil, divided

2 lb boneless bison chuck roast (such as blade, cross-rib, or shoulder), cut into 1½-inch cubes and patted dry

2 Vidalia onions or other sweet onions, chopped

4 cloves garlic, minced

12 oz cremini mushrooms, sliced

1 cup chardonnay

1 (14 oz) can diced tomatoes

1 cup bison, beef, chicken, or vegetable stock

4 sprigs fresh thyme

1 tsp kosher salt

1 tsp freshly ground black pepper

2 cups trimmed and chopped Swiss chard

This reminds me of the Scotch broth soup I adored growing up. Soups are flexible and forgiving. Bison and pot barley (which isn't as processed as pearl barley) are essential, but use whatever vegetables and fresh herbs you have on hand. No fresh herbs? Add 1 to 2 tablespoons of mixed dried spices when you're softening the vegetables. Cut everything in a small dice. This makes a big batch and freezes well.

Bison Barley Soup

Makes about 10 servings

In a large saucepan or stockpot over medium-high, heat 1 tablespoon of the oil. Add the bison. Cook until browned, about 6 minutes. Add the remaining 1 tablespoon of oil and the bell peppers, celery, onion, carrot, potato, corn, and garlic. Cook, stirring, for 5 minutes to soften.

Add the water, diced tomatoes with their juices, tomato paste, and barley. Stir well. Raise the heat to high and bring to a boil. Reduce the heat to low and cover. Cook, stirring occasionally, until the meat is tender, barley is plump, and soup thickens slightly, about 2 hours. Season with salt and pepper. Stir in the herbs.

2 Tbsp canola oil, divided

1 to 2 lb boneless bison stewing meat, diced and patted dry

3 bell peppers (mix of red, orange, yellow, or green), diced

2 stalks celery, diced

1 medium yellow onion, diced

1 large carrot, peeled and diced

1 Yukon Gold or yellow-fleshed potato, diced

1 cup fresh or frozen corn

4 large cloves garlic, minced

8 cups water

1 (28 oz) can diced tomatoes

1 (5½ oz) can tomato paste

1 cup dried pot barley, rinsed

Kosher salt

Freshly ground black pepper

½ cup mixed chopped fresh herbs (such as rosemary, thyme, flat-leaf parsley, and cilantro)

There's no fresh corn in this riff on an American classic known as Frito pie, but the flavor comes through thanks to corn chips and cornmeal or masa harina, a corn flour that's used to make tortillas and tamales. I buy Maseca brand, which can be found in Latin American grocery stores and the Mexican/international area of supermarkets.

Bison Corn Pie with Tortilla Chips

Makes 4 to 6 servings

In a large nonstick skillet over medium-high, heat 1 tablespoon of the oil. Add the bison (or in batches if necessary). Cook for 6 minutes to brown. Add the ancho powder, cumin, and oregano. Cook, stirring, for 1 minute. Transfer the bison to a plate. Add the remaining 2 tablespoons of oil to the skillet and heat over medium. Add the onions, garlic, and jalapeno. Cook, stirring, for 6 minutes to soften.

Transfer the onion mixture to a large saucepan. Add the reserved bison and any juices. Cover with 2 inches of water. Bring to a boil over high heat, and then reduce the heat to low and cover. Simmer for 90 minutes. Stir in the cornmeal or masa harina to thicken. Simmer, covered, for 30 minutes or until the meat is fork-tender.

Serve the corn pie in bowls with tortilla or corn chips on the side. If you like, top it with cheese, jalapenos, and sour cream.

3 Tbsp canola oil, divided

3 lb bison stewing meat, cut into bite-size chunks and patted dry

3 Tbsp ancho chili powder

1 Tbsp ground cumin

1 Tbsp dried oregano leaves

2 medium yellow onions, finely diced

5 large cloves garlic, minced

1 large jalapeno, seeded and minced

3 Tbsp fine cornmeal or masa harina (instant white or yellow Mexican corn flour)

Tortilla or corn chips

OPTIONAL TOPPINGS:
Grated cheddar
Chopped jalapenos
Sour cream

Like all stews, this one tastes even better if you can make it a day ahead of time. Warm it gently in a saucepan before making the dumplings and finishing the cooking. Look for Maseca brand masa harina in the international aisle or Mexican area of supermarkets.

Ancho Bison Stew with Corn Dumplings

Makes 6 servings

For the stew, season the bison to taste with salt and pepper.

In a large, wide pot or a deep, wide skillet, heat 2 tablespoons of the oil. Add the bison in batches. Cook until browned all over, about 5 minutes. Transfer to a bowl.

Heat the remaining 1 tablespoon of oil in the same pan over medium. Add the onions and garlic. Cook, stirring, for 5 minutes. Stir in the ancho powder, cumin, and oregano. Cook, stirring, for 1 minute. Stir in the chipotle purée. Cook, stirring, for 2 minutes. Add the reserved bison with its juices, and the water. Raise the heat to high and bring to a boil. Reduce the heat to low and cover. Simmer, stirring occasionally and adding water if needed, for 2 hours or until fork-tender. Stir in the cilantro.

For the dumplings, in a bowl, stir together the masa harina, all-purpose flour, baking powder, baking soda, and salt. Mix in the butter using your fingers until the mixture resembles coarse crumbs. Add the buttermilk. Stir gently to just moisten.

Remove the lid from the simmering stew. Dollop the dumpling dough by heaping tablespoonfuls on top of the stew. Reduce the heat to low and cover. Cook until the tops of the dumplings are dry, about 15 to 20 minutes.

STEW:

3 lb boneless bison stewing meat, chopped and patted dry

Kosher salt

Freshly ground black pepper

3 Tbsp canola oil, divided

2 medium yellow onions, chopped

5 cloves garlic, minced

2 Tbsp ancho chili powder

1 Tbsp ground cumin

1 Tbsp dried oregano leaves

3 Tbsp puréed canned chipotle chilies packed in adobo sauce (see Cooking Tip, p. 32)

4 cups water

¼ cup chopped cilantro

DUMPLINGS:

¾ cup masa harina (instant white Mexican corn flour)

¼ cup all-purpose flour

1 tsp baking powder

¼ tsp baking soda

¼ tsp kosher salt

¼ cup cold unsalted butter, cut into pieces

¾ cup well-shaken buttermilk

Ever since I interviewed an Ontario sweet potato farmer and tramped around his field, I've enjoyed a healthy addiction to the sweet orange-fleshed tubers, which are often mislabeled as yams. This nutrient-dense, colorful stew comes from Peter J. Duffin, who passionately advocates for grass-fed bison at his recipe website, bisonbasics.com.

Sweet Potato + Sweet Pea Bison Stew

Makes 6 to 8 servings

Put the flour in a large, shallow bowl. Add the bison cubes, tossing to coat well. Discard the excess flour.

In a large saucepan over medium-high, heat 2 tablespoons of the oil. Add the bison, in batches if needed, and brown, about 6 minutes. Transfer to a plate. Add the remaining 2 tablespoons of oil to the pan, along with the onions and garlic. Cook, stirring often, for 6 minutes to soften. Add the bison, water, paprika, salt, pepper, and basil. Raise the heat to high and bring to a boil, and then reduce the heat to low and cover. Simmer for 2 hours or until the bison is tender. Add the carrots and sweet potatoes. Cover and simmer for 30 minutes or until the vegetables are tender but not mushy. Stir in the peas. Simmer for 5 minutes.

If you prefer to use a slow cooker, transfer the bison to it after the meat has been browned. You won't need the second 2 tablespoons of oil. Add the onions, garlic, water, paprika, salt, pepper, basil, carrots, and sweet potatoes. Cover and cook according to the manufacturer's instructions, on low or high as desired, until the meat is fork-tender. Add the peas during the last 30 minutes of cooking.

½ cup all-purpose flour

2 lb boneless bison stewing meat, cut into bite-size cubes and patted dry

4 Tbsp extra-virgin olive oil, divided

2 medium yellow onions, halved and thinly sliced

3 large cloves garlic, minced

4 cups water

1 tsp paprika

1 tsp kosher salt

½ tsp freshly ground black pepper

½ tsp dried basil

2 large carrots, peeled and chopped

1½ lb sweet potatoes, peeled and chopped

1½ cups frozen peas

Peter and Judy Haase run Buffalo Horn Ranch (buffalohornranch.ca) near Eagle Hill, Alberta, northwest of Calgary. This is "one of our favorite meals after a day outside, whether we are working buffalo in the corrals or cross-country skiing." Peter calls himself a rustic, seasonal cook who grows his own tomatoes and potatoes, and makes his own beer. However you get your ingredients, serve this stew with hearty bread and a salad.

Buffalo Horn Ranch's Bison Stew

Makes 4 to 6 servings

In a large, heavy skillet over medium-high, heat 1 tablespoon of the oil. In two batches, cook the meat until browned, about 6 minutes. Transfer the meat to a slow cooker or a large pot. Add the remaining 2 tablespoons of oil to the skillet. Add the onions, carrots, and garlic. Cook, stirring, for 5 minutes to soften. Sprinkle with the rosemary, powdered mustard, cumin, and coriander. Cook, stirring, for 2 minutes. Transfer to the slow cooker or pot.

Add the tomatoes with their juices and the beer to the skillet. Cook, scraping up any browned bits and breaking up the tomatoes with a wooden spoon. When the mixture begins to boil, pour it into the slow cooker or pot. Add the potatoes, chili, bay leaf, and molasses to the slow cooker or pot. If using a slow cooker, cook according to manufacturer's instructions, on high or low as desired. Alternately, if using a pot on the stove, bring the stew to a boil over high heat, and then reduce the heat to low and cover. Simmer until tender, about 3 to 5 hours. Season to taste with salt and pepper.

3 Tbsp extra-virgin olive oil, divided

1 lb boneless bison stewing meat, cut into 1-inch cubes and patted dry

2 medium yellow onions, chopped

2 large carrots, peeled and chopped

3 large cloves garlic, chopped

1 tsp chopped fresh rosemary

1 tsp powdered mustard

½ tsp ground cumin

½ tsp ground coriander

1 (19 oz) can whole tomatoes, or 1 lb fresh tomatoes, chopped

1 (11½ oz) bottle dark ale or stout (such as Big Rock Black Amber Ale or Guinness)

1 lb yellow-fleshed potatoes, cut into 1-inch chunks

1 dried chili pepper (any kind and size), stemmed and crushed

1 bay leaf

1 Tbsp molasses

Kosher salt

Freshly ground black pepper

Celebrating White Bison

If you're ever lucky enough to see a white bison, just enjoy it. It's a rare and beautiful creature to behold no matter how it came to be on this Earth.

You see, there are four overlapping possible explanations for the phenomenon. Many white bison are actually beefalo. Some are albino bison. Scientists say a small percentage of these rarities—maybe 1 in 10 million—could be white because of a rare surfacing of a recessive mutation that leaves the hair follicles without melanin. First Nations peoples believe white bison are a sacred symbol, powerful spirit, and good omen.

I've seen four white bison. Three were beefalo, a bison-beef cattle crossbreed. The fourth, I'd like to believe, was the mystical kind.

His name is Blizzard, and he lives at the Assiniboine Park Zoo in Winnipeg, Manitoba, with three brown bison cows and some white-tailed deer. I meet Blizzard, so to speak, on a summer day from behind the fence that separates the zoo's bison enclosure from its public parking lot.

Dr. Robert Wrigley drives me to the parking lot for a quick visit. Bob, formerly the zoo curator, brought Blizzard here during a 2006 snowstorm when the animal was just a year old. A gift from an anonymous American rancher, Blizzard was the first white bison to make a splash in Manitoba, where the provincial symbol is actually a bison.

"There's Blizzard right there," says Bob excitedly, pointing through the fence to an otherworldly animal with a cloak of white hair grazing serenely in the center of a field. "He really cooperates. Anytime you need to do something, he's right there. If I had a pail of alfalfa pellets, I'd just shake it and he'd come at a gallop."

Unfortunately, Bob retired in 2011, so we can't draw Blizzard to us with food. Besides, the warning sign says, "For the safety and security of our animals, please do not feed them."

You may not be allowed feed them, but you can still honor them. I'm intrigued by a couple of small cloth bundles tied to the fence. One is yellow, tied with brown yarn. The other is blue with blue yarn. Bob knows what they are but gets all mysterious about the answer.

We say goodbye to Blizzard—who doesn't come close enough for a good look anyway—and drive to the Health Sciences Centre to speak to spiritual health specialist Roger Armitte.

Roger has time for a break, so we chat in the cafeteria over sandwiches. "Those cloth bundles would have been tobacco offerings," the Ojibwa elder says. "People would have been acknowledging the spirit of the buffalo and perhaps giving thanks for something that happened. Overall, it's a sign of respect. The color of the cloth would have been significant to the person or the family."

Buffalo have always been very important to First Nations peoples, who still call them buffalo, not bison. "One of the elders said a buffalo is actually our very first shopping mall," continues Roger, "because they provided everything—food, medicine, clothing, fuel, lodging, protection. It was seen as a provider."

The white buffalo is considered a powerful spirit in First Nations Plains culture, to the Dakota, Lakota, and other tribes. In the legend of the White Buffalo Calf Woman, the Great Spirit appears as a woman, dressed in white buckskin, who gives a sacred pipe, and the gifts of knowledge, food, and prayer, to the suffering Lakota people. As she leaves, she turns into a white buffalo calf.

First Nations peoples honor white buffalo with ceremonies and prayers. They consider them good omens and a sign of renewal.

Back in 2006 as Blizzard waited out his first few months in Winnipeg in quarantine, word filtered out about his existence. Bob got a call from an elder who said, "You have no idea what you've got here as far as the First Nations is concerned. We want to ensure proper protocol is respected."

Blizzard was welcomed with a ceremony full of singing, dancing, drumming, and smudging.

DR. ROBERT WRIGLEY AND A TOBACCO OFFERING

"Through that whole ceremony, that buffalo was right there as close as the distance now from you to me," says Roger. "Remember that?" he asks Bob. "That was something."

Until Blizzard's arrival, First Nations communities rarely visited the zoo. The zoo created signs about Blizzard and the white buffalo legend in Cree, Ojibwa, Dene, and Dakota. Elders were allowed to build a sweat lodge near the buffalo field and used it to welcome new police recruits taking Aboriginal sensitivity training. Bob sometimes took First Nations visitors to a private nook to feed Blizzard grass through the fence, a small gesture that was of great spiritual importance. First Nations school groups started visiting. People made pilgrimages from across North America.

"The white buffalo brought people together," recalls Roger, "which in tradition is what it was meant to do."

The people may have instantly adored Blizzard, but his fellow buffalo (all female) gave

ROGER ARMITTE

him a rough ride at first. "When he tried to follow the girls and say, 'I'm one of the group,' they'd say 'Back off, I'm not ready for that,'" recalls Dr. Chris Enright, the zoo's head of veterinary services. "They let him know his place was sort of on the periphery."

Eventually, Blizzard was accepted. Although he was brought to the zoo for cultural reasons, he was allowed to breed once and produced three calves with three mothers. They were white, off-white, and brown. The white and brown calves were given to the Sioux Valley Dakota Nation as a gift from the zoo and the City of Winnipeg, which ran the zoo until turning it over to a non-profit conservancy a few years ago.

Blizzard was once loaned to the Calgary Zoo for five months. First Nations elders there treated him to a special transfer ceremony and gave him an Aboriginal name.

Roger still visits once a week. Bob credits Blizzard with "really opening my eyes to a completely different culture of which I knew very little."

Blizzard is now a mature bull in his prime with nothing to prove. "Calm, cool, and collected" is how Chris describes him. "He's kind of tall and gangly and he's always been that way. He's a big puppy dog. He's definitely the most people-oriented bison that we have."

Blizzard eats grass, hay, grain-based pellets, browse (tree cuttings), and an occasional biscuit treat designed for leaf eaters. He can wander his outdoor enclosure, or go into an unheated barn at night and curl up on the straw.

Many white bison eventually turn brown, like Yellow Medicine Dancing Boy, who lives at the Mohawk Bison Farm in Connecticut and has drawn countless Native American visitors.

I've read about three albino bison—White Cloud, Dakota Miracle, and Dakota Legend—that are part of the herd at the National Buffalo Museum in North Dakota.

Native Americans were instrumental in having a "near-white" buffalo (actually a beefalo) moved to the Fort Worth Nature Center and Refuge in Texas from a gas station where she was treated as a sideshow while pregnant. Although they didn't consider her a sacred white buffalo, they felt she was still symbolic.

The three other white buffalo that I have seen were at Ivan Smith's ranch just outside of Red Deer, Alberta. The bull, cow, and calf were there briefly while on government quarantine, as they passed from an American owner to a Canadian owner.

That Canadian owner turns out to be Rudy Deutsch. He is 91 and has amassed a herd of 16 white bison near Sylvan Lake, Alberta, over the past three years. With help from his son and daughter-in-law, he hopes to breed what he calls "the bison hybrid" (not beefalo) for trophy hunts, pets (for a place in Texas), and meat, which he will market as "Divine Beef."

"They've got so much to offer, it's unbelievable," says Rudy. "We could revolutionize the beef industry with that little herd of mine."

I try to find a white-buffalo expert and turn to Saskatchewan bison specialist Wes Olson, a retired Parks Canada warden who has written several bison books. Having never seen a white bison in more than 30 years working with the animals, he traveled to the Calgary Zoo to see Blizzard, who hid in a far corner of the pasture and was barely visible.

"I often contemplated what it would be like should a white calf arrive in one of the populations I've worked with," admits Wes. "I invariably shudder and hope it does not happen, simply because of the intense focus the animal would be under and the logistics involved in ensuring that nothing happened to it. On the other hand, they are extremely rare in the wild, so knowing one exists is also pretty special, and I too would go out of my way to have a peek at one."

The nuances of how each of these white buffalo that I've met or read about came to be don't interest Roger Armitte. "It's amazing the number of white buffalo that are coming," he says, thrilled to hear about all of them. "What is the reason? Maybe it's the time of the awakening. See, most tribes, actually all tribes, in their prophecies speak of a time of awakening and messengers that are sent to prepare the people for that."

Blizzard the messenger. It sounds right.

Chapter 5

Ribs/Shanks

I swear by my slow cooker for cooking bison ribs and shanks. Treat these bony beauties like less tender roasts (aka pot roasts). Season them, rub them with oil, and sear them in a skillet over medium-high so they get brown and crusty. Then toss them in a slow cooker with lots of liquid (wine, beer, stock, water, juice, canned tomatoes) and let them cook until the meat is falling off the bone. If you don't have a slow cooker, put them in a Dutch oven or heavy pot, cover them, and braise them in an oven preheated to 300°F. Cook them a day ahead if possible for extra deliciousness. Reheat them in their braising liquid.

Your butcher can cut back ribs and short ribs. Back ribs are pretty straightforward and come in a rack. But there are multiple ways to butcher short ribs. They can be cut as Texas ribs, which are actually long single ribs. They can be cut as short single ribs, about 2 to 3 inches long. Yet another option is thin and crosscut, with three or four bones showing. These might be called Maui-style or Korean- or galbi-style ribs.

If you leave your cooked meat on the bones, you're limited in your portions. To extend the portions, you can discard the bones before serving and chop up the meat. Or you can shred the meat and serve it bathed in its braising liquid.

Shanks are the part of the leg between the knee and the ankle. For most bison, only the meatier back shanks are used. They can be left huge and whole. They can be cut crosswise into two pieces. Or they can be crosscut osso buco–style so you can see (and eat!) the delicious marrow in the center of the bone.

You can mix and match any style of rib or shank for the recipes in this chapter. Some ribs are meatier than others, and some have a higher ratio of bones to meat, so the portion sizes are estimates.

Kansas City barbecue pairs slow-cooked meat with a tomato and molasses barbecue sauce that's thick, sweet, spicy, and tangy. Ted's Montana Grill (tedsmontanagrill.com) replicates this flavor profile with its saucy braised ribs. Corporate chef Chris Raucci shared this recipe, and I've streamlined it. His short ribs are cut in four-bone slabs that weigh about 1 pound before cooking and 8 ounces after cooking. Use whatever spice blend you like, or even just kosher salt and black pepper. Chris serves his restaurant ribs with garlic mashed potatoes and green beans.

Braised Bison Short Ribs in Barbecue Sauce

Makes 8 servings

Preheat the oven to 400°F.

Pour the oil into a large roasting pan. Heat the pan, uncovered, for 10 minutes.

Season the ribs with the spice blend. Place half of the ribs, meat side down, in the hot oil without crowding. Sear in the oven for 5 minutes. Turn the ribs over. Sear on the bone side for 5 minutes. Transfer the ribs to a plate. Repeat this process with the remaining ribs. (If you prefer, sear your ribs in a large skillet over medium-high heat on the stove.) Return all of the seared ribs to the pan, with the meaty sides facing down.

In a mixing bowl or 8-cup measuring cup, stir together the water, 1 cup of the barbecue sauce, and the tomato paste, bouillon, liquid smoke, and bay leaves. Pour over the ribs. Cover the pan with the lid or with foil. Reduce the oven temperature to 300°F. Cook until the meat is very tender, about 3½ to 4 hours.

With tongs, transfer the ribs to a plate and let them cool for about 10 minutes. When cool enough to handle, gently pull off and discard the fatty tissue from the top layer of each rib.

Meanwhile, for the sauce, transfer the cooking liquid to a large pot. Add the remaining 2 cups of barbecue sauce. Bring to a boil over high heat.

¼ cup canola oil

8 lb bison short ribs (about 8), rinsed and patted dry

1 Tbsp Ted Turner's Special Spice Mixture (see p. 31), or your favorite spice blend

6 cups water

3 cups barbecue sauce (preferably Cattlemen's Kansas City Classic), divided

¼ cup tomato paste

2 Tbsp liquid beef bouillon concentrate

1 Tbsp liquid smoke

2 bay leaves

¾ cup all-purpose flour (optional)

1 cup cold water (optional)

If you want your sauce to be thicker, in a small mixing bowl, whisk the flour and cold water until smooth. Slowly whisk the flour mixture into the boiling liquid (if you do it too quickly, it will be very lumpy). Simmer for 5 minutes until the sauce thickens.

Return the ribs to the sauce if they need to be warmed. Serve the ribs smothered in sauce.

Ted Turner—Bison Mogul

Ted Turner is doing more for bison than anyone else in the world. You heard that right—billionaire environmentalist Ted Turner, the media mogul and founder of CNN, is also the world's largest bison rancher. He cofounded Ted's Montana Grill, a chain that serves about 2 million pounds (900,000 kilograms) of bison per year and boasts the biggest bison menu of any restaurant.

Ted's unexpected passion for bison is detailed in a great book called *Last Stand: Ted Turner's Quest to Save a Troubled Planet* (Lyons Press, 2013) by Todd Wilkinson. In fact, the first chapter is called "Empire of Bison." According to tedturner.com, Ted is the second-largest individual landowner in North America with about 2 million acres (800,000 hectares). He bought his first bison in 1976 and now raises more than 55,000 of them on 14 of his 15 ranches in seven western states.

More importantly, Ted created a restaurant company to help preserve bison by bringing it back to the table. In 2002, he and restaurateur George McKerrow Jr. launched Ted's Montana Grill, an upscale Old West chain specializing in bison. At last count, there were 44 restaurants in 16 states—but sadly none yet in Canada. The chain's mantra is "Eat great. Do good." Not only is TMG responsible for encouraging millions of people to try bison, it provides incentive for ranchers to grow their herds since the chain supplements Ted's meat with meat from other ranchers.

Bison accounts for about 40 percent of menu sales. There are burgers, steaks, short ribs, pot roast, meatloaf, and chili. "I knew that if people tried it and if it was prepared properly, they would like it," says Ted on the chain's website. Corporate chef Chris Raucci shared three recipes for this cookbook. Look for burgers on page 30, chili on page 60, and short ribs on page 162.

Anchos—which are dried poblano chili peppers—are sweet and mild. You can buy them whole, soak them in hot water, and chop them up, but an easier ground powder is widely available in supermarkets. I make these ribs in a slow cooker, starting out for 1 hour on high heat and then switching to low for at least 6 hours. You'll want to serve this feast on mashed root vegetables or creamy polenta to soak up the braising liquid.

Ancho-Dusted Bison Ribs with Rustic Mixed Mash

Makes 4 to 6 servings

Leave your ribs as is if they're single, meaty short ribs, or cut them Maui-, Korean-, or galbi-style through the bone so that there are several rib eyes showing with each meaty piece. If your back ribs come in racks, remove any silver skin or connective tissue and then cut into individual ribs.

In a small bowl, stir together the ancho powder, cinnamon, salt, and pepper. Rub this spice mixture all over the ribs.

Preheat the oven to 300°F.

Heat 3 tablespoons of oil in a large ovenproof pot over medium-high heat. Cook the ribs, in batches, until browned, about 3 minutes per side. Add more oil if needed. Transfer the ribs to a plate. Add the onion, carrots, celery, and garlic to the pot. Cook, stirring, for 6 minutes to soften. Add the wine and stock or water. Bring to a simmer. Return the ribs to the pot. Cover and cook until the meat is tender and almost falling off the bone, about 3 to 4 hours. Stir in the thyme.

Alternately, once you've browned the meat, transfer it to a slow cooker. Top with the onion, carrots, celery, and garlic. Pour the wine and stock or water over everything. Cook according to the manufacturer's instructions, on low or high heat as desired, until fork-tender. Sprinkle with the thyme.

To serve, strain the meat and vegetables and transfer them to a serving dish. Pass the braising liquid separately. (You may want to transfer the liquid to a small saucepan and boil for a few minutes to thicken to desired consistency.)

Serve with the mixed mash, if desired.

3 lb bison short or back ribs, rinsed and patted dry

3 Tbsp ancho chili powder

2 tsp ground cinnamon

2 tsp kosher salt

2 tsp freshly ground black pepper

3 Tbsp canola oil

1 large yellow onion, halved and thinly sliced

2 carrots, peeled and chopped

1 stalk celery, chopped

3 large cloves garlic, minced

2 cups dry red wine (such as merlot)

2 cups bison or beef stock or water

2 Tbsp fresh thyme leaves

Rustic Mixed Mash (optional, see opposite page)

I like my mashes simple and rustic. I start with potatoes—unpeeled—and add parsnips or carrots for sweetness. I don't gild the lily with butter, milk, or cream, and I don't mash until smooth and glossy. I figure I'm putting beautiful bison on top of my mashes, and a flavorful sauce or braising liquid, so I don't need any frills.

Rustic Mixed Mash

Makes about 3½ cups (for about 6 servings)

Put the potatoes, parsnips, and carrots in a large pot, and fill with water. Bring to a boil over high heat. Boil until the vegetables are very tender, about 15 to 20 minutes.

Scoop out 1 cup of the cooking liquid and reserve, and then drain well. Return the vegetables to the pot. Add a ¼ cup of the reserved cooking liquid. Mash with a potato masher or fork, drizzling in more cooking liquid as needed to reach desired texture. If you're serving this with ribs or shanks and sauce, you don't need to season it. Otherwise, season to taste with salt and pepper.

1 lb Yukon Gold or yellow-fleshed potatoes (about 2 large), peeled, if desired, and chopped

8 oz parsnips, peeled and chopped

8 oz carrots, peeled and chopped

Kosher salt

Freshly ground black pepper

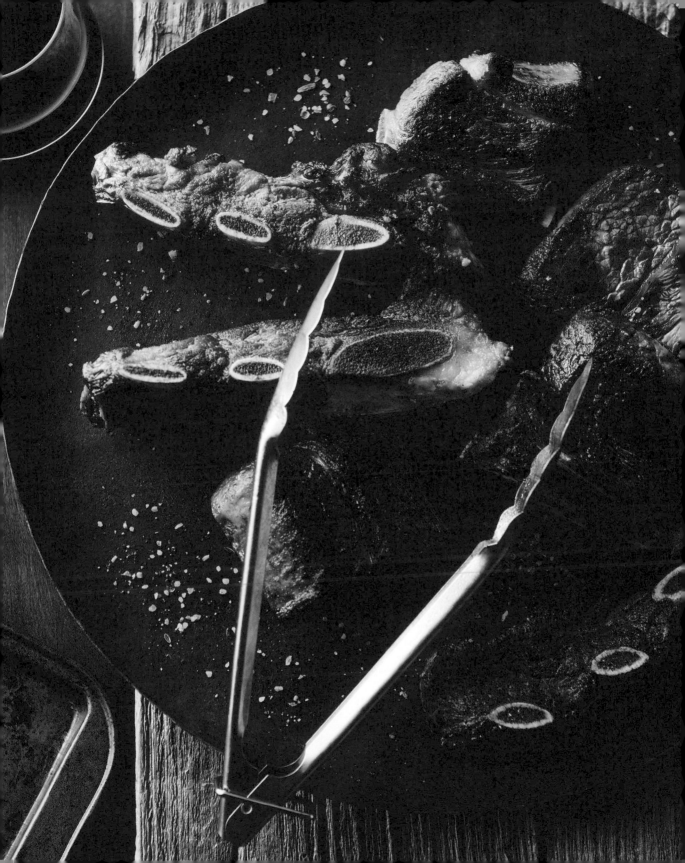

Guinness used to be my default dark beer for cooking, but there are so many great craft beers now that you can always find something made locally. I am particularly fond of oatmeal stouts and coffee porters.

Beer-Braised Bison Ribs with a Chipotle Kick

Makes 4 to 6 servings

If using the oven, preheat to 300°F.

Leave your ribs as is if they're single, meaty short ribs, or cut them Maui-, Korean-, or galbi-style through the bone so that there are several rib eyes showing with each meaty piece. If your back ribs come in racks, remove any silver skin or connective tissue and then cut into individual ribs.

Stir together the salt and pepper. Rub all over the ribs. Rub the ribs with oil.

Heat a large skillet over medium-high. Add the ribs. Cook until well browned, about 2 to 3 minutes. Transfer to a slow cooker or ovenproof pot or roasting pan.

In a mixing bowl or measuring cup, stir together the beer, honey, soy sauce, and chipotle purée or powder. Pour over the ribs.

If using the oven, cover the pot and cook until tender, about 3 to 4 hours. For the slow cooker, cook according to the manufacturer's instructions, on low or high as desired, until tender.

Serve the ribs covered with the braising liquid, or pass the liquid separately.

3 lb bison short or back ribs, rinsed and patted dry

2 Tbsp kosher salt

1 Tbsp freshly ground black pepper

Extra-virgin olive oil

1 (11½ oz) bottle dark beer (such as a stout or porter)

¼ cup honey

¼ cup soy sauce

2 Tbsp puréed canned chipotle chilies packed in adobo sauce (see Cooking Tip, p. 32), or 1 Tbsp ground chipotle powder

If you've enjoyed galbi (grilled beef short ribs) at a Korean restaurant, you'll recognize these flavors. It's a little harder to get bison ribs cut this way, but ask for Maui-style or Korean- or galbi-style. They're cut across the bone into long, thin strips.

Garlic-Soy Bison Ribs

Makes 4 to 6 servings

Leave your ribs as is if they're single, meaty short ribs, or cut them Maui-, Korean-, or galbi-style through the bone so that there are several rib eyes showing with each meaty piece. If your back ribs come in racks, remove any silver skin or connective tissue and then cut into individual ribs.

In a mixing bowl or measuring cup, combine the pear, onion, garlic, ginger, soy sauce, sugar, sesame oil, and pepper. Stir well. Pour into a large resealable plastic bag. Add the ribs, turning to coat. Refrigerate, turning occasionally, for at least 6 hours but preferably overnight.

Preheat the oven to 300°F.

Transfer the ribs and marinade to a large Dutch oven or oven-proof pot or roasting pan. Cover and cook until fork-tender, about 3 to 4 hours, adding water if needed. Remove the ribs from the liquid to serve.

3 lb bison short or back ribs, preferably cut galbi-style, rinsed and patted dry

1 Asian pear, peeled, cored, and grated

1 medium yellow onion, chopped

6 large cloves garlic, minced

1 tsp peeled and minced ginger

½ cup dark soy sauce

¼ cup granulated sugar

1 Tbsp Asian sesame oil

1 tsp freshly ground black pepper

I was lucky enough to visit Thailand three times while living overseas. I was young and traveled on a budget as a backpacker. Most meals were simple red or green curries with vegetables and a bit of chicken. I now pair red curry and bison a lot. Inspiration for this dish comes from *Eating Well* magazine, which did a feature on bison in 2009.

Thai Red Curry Bison Ribs

Makes 4 to 6 servings

Leave your ribs as is if they're single, meaty short ribs, or cut them Maui-, Korean-, or galbi-style through the bone so that there are several rib eyes showing with each meaty piece. If your back ribs come in racks, remove any silver skin or connective tissue and then cut into individual ribs.

Preheat the oven to 300°F.

In a food processor or blender, combine the curry paste, garlic, ginger, ½ cup of the cilantro, green onions, and ½ cup of the water. Blend to a loose paste, adding more water if needed to loosen the mixture.

In a large ovenproof pot over medium-high, heat the oil. Add the ribs, in batches if necessary, and brown all over, about 6 minutes. Stir in the red curry mixture, the remaining 2 cups of water, and the lime juice. Scatter the yellow onions over everything.

Cover and cook until the meat is fork-tender, about 3 to 4 hours. Transfer the ribs to a plate. Cover loosely with foil. When cool enough to handle, shred the meat, discarding the bones and any fat.

To the braising liquid, add the tomatoes, the coconut milk, and the remaining ½ cup of cilantro. Place on the stove over medium-high heat. Bring to a boil and then reduce the heat to medium and simmer for 10 minutes. Stir in the shredded meat.

Serve the red curry bison with jasmine rice.

3 lb bison short or back ribs, rinsed and patted dry

1 Tbsp Thai red curry paste

4 large cloves garlic, chopped

1 Tbsp peeled and minced ginger

1 cup chopped cilantro, divided

6 green onions, chopped

2½ cups water, divided

1 Tbsp canola oil

Juice of 1 lime

2 medium yellow onions, halved and thinly sliced

4 Roma (plum) tomatoes, seeded and diced

1 cup canned coconut milk

Cooked jasmine rice, for serving

This is a popular dish at the Bison Restaurant & Terrace (thebison.ca) in Banff, Alberta. Executive chef Liz Gagnon serves the short ribs atop roasted vegetables in a small cast-iron skillet for a "campy/rustic" feel. She also uses a wood-burning oven "to add that extra touch of deliciousness."

The Bison Restaurant's Bison Short Ribs with Roasted Vegetables

Makes 4 to 6 servings

Leave your ribs as is if they're single, meaty short ribs, or cut them Maui-, Korean-, or galbi-style through the bone so that there are several rib eyes showing with each meaty piece. If your back ribs come in racks, remove any silver skin or connective tissue and then cut into individual ribs.

In a small bowl, stir together the salt, pepper, garlic powder, and paprika. Rub all over the ribs.

Preheat the oven to 300°F.

Preheat a large, heavy roasting pan over medium-high until smoking. Add the oil. In two batches, carefully add the ribs. Cook until darkly caramelized all over, about 8 to 10 minutes. Transfer to a bowl. Add the onions, carrots, and celery to the pan. Cook, stirring, for 7 minutes until well browned. Add the wine and stock. Cook, stirring up any browned bits. Bring to a boil. Add the ribs and any juices to the pan, along with the rosemary, thyme, and bay leaves.

Cover the pan with foil or a lid and place in the oven. Cook until the meat is tender and just falling off the bones, about 3 to 4 hours. Transfer the ribs to a bowl. Strain the braising liquid into a medium saucepan, discarding the solids. Boil over high heat until reduced by half.

Serve the short ribs with the roasted vegetables, if desired. Pour the braising reduction overtop. Garnish with the herbs, if desired.

4 lb bison short or back ribs, rinsed and patted dry

1 Tbsp kosher salt

1 Tbsp freshly ground black pepper

1 Tbsp garlic powder

1 Tbsp paprika

2 Tbsp canola oil

2 medium yellow onions, chopped

3 large carrots, peeled and chopped

3 stalks celery, chopped

1 (25.4 oz) bottle red wine (preferably Syrah or Burgundy)

3 cups bison or beef stock

3 sprigs fresh rosemary

3 sprigs fresh thyme

3 bay leaves

OPTIONAL ACCOMPANIMENTS:

The Bison Restaurant's Roasted Vegetables (see opposite page)

Chopped fresh rosemary, thyme, or flat-leaf parsley

These are the roasted vegetables that the Bison Restaurant serves with its short ribs. Executive chef Liz Gagnon says the trick is to cut everything the same size, so keep everything to the size of the pearl onions and mini potatoes. If you don't want to use bacon, season with kosher salt and use extra oil. Personally, I don't love turnips, so I would substitute a couple of sweet parsnips.

The Bison Restaurant's Roasted Vegetables

Makes 4 to 6 servings

Preheat the oven to 400°F.

Bring a medium saucepan of water to boil over high heat. Add the pearl onions. Cook for 1 minute, and then drain and transfer to a bowl of ice water to stop the cooking. Let cool for a couple of minutes, and then pinch the stem ends of the onions—they should slip out of their skins. (If they need a little help, use a paring knife.)

In a large mixing bowl, combine the pearl onions, potatoes, mushrooms, carrots, turnip, bacon, and oil. Sprinkle with pepper to taste. Toss well.

Spread the vegetables in a single layer on a large rimmed baking sheet or in a roasting pan. Roast until tender, stirring once or twice, about 45 to 55 minutes.

12 pearl onions, root ends trimmed

16 mini red potatoes (about 12 oz)

6 cremini mushrooms, halved

2 carrots, peeled and cut into 1-inch chunks

1 small turnip (about 4 oz), peeled and cut into 1-inch chunks

6 slices double-smoked bacon, chopped

1 Tbsp extra-virgin olive oil

Freshly ground black pepper

" I like bison because it's something different than what everybody else has. We get a lot of tourists from the States and Europe. A lot of people come here just to try bison. It's just delicious, so you don't really need to mess with it too much. You can let the flavor of the meat shine with each recipe." —Liz Gagnon

"This dish is done with a hint of the Old West, or mole style, south of the border, with a Tex-Mex flare," says Frederick Clabaugh, executive chef of Tenaya Lodge (tenayalodge.com) at Yosemite in Fish Camp, California. These ribs cry out for polenta, grits, or mashed potatoes to mop up the rich sauce. Mexican chocolate tablets are spiced with cinnamon and sugar. Frederick prefers Ibarra brand, but Abuelita is also popular, and any brand will do. Look for them in Latin American grocery stores or the Mexican area of mainstream supermarkets.

Southwestern Braised Bison Short Ribs

Makes 6 to 8 servings

Generously season the ribs with salt.

In a large ovenproof pot over medium-high, heat 2 tablespoons of the oil. Add the ribs, in batches, and brown very well, about 3 minutes per side. Transfer the ribs to a plate. If needed, drain any fat.

Preheat the oven to 300°F.

In a food processor, combine the onion, celery, carrots, and garlic. Pulse into a coarse paste. Add to the pot, along with the remaining 2 tablespoons of oil. Cook, stirring frequently, over medium-high heat, until the vegetable paste turns brown and a crust forms on the bottom of the pot, about 7 to 10 minutes. Scrape the crust and let it reform. Scrape the crust again.

Add the tomato paste. Cook, stirring, until brown, about 4 to 5 minutes. Add the wine. Stir up any browned bits and lower the heat if things start to burn. Cook until the liquid is reduced by half. Return the ribs to the pot. Add water to just cover the meat. Add the thyme bundle, Mexican or Tex-Mex seasoning, coffee beans, chocolate, and bay leaves.

Cover the pot and transfer it to the oven. Cook, checking occasionally to turn the meat and add more water if needed, until the ribs are very tender, about 3 to 4 hours. Remove the lid during the last 20 minutes of cooking to let the meat brown and the sauce thicken.

Continued on page 174

5 to 6 lb bison short ribs, rinsed and patted dry

Kosher salt

4 Tbsp extra-virgin olive oil, divided

1 large Spanish onion or other sweet onion, chopped

2 stalks celery, chopped

2 carrots, peeled, halved lengthwise, and chopped

2 cloves garlic, smashed

1½ cups tomato paste (about 3 [5½ oz] cans)

1 (25.4 oz) bottle hearty red wine

1 bunch fresh thyme, tied with kitchen twine

¼ cup Tex-Mex spice blend or homemade taco seasoning

¼ cup whole coffee beans

2 oz Mexican spiced chocolate tablets (such as Ibarra), chopped

2 bay leaves

Continued from page 172

Transfer the ribs to a platter.

Pass the braising liquid through a strainer, discarding the bay leaves and coffee beans. If desired, place the liquid in a medium saucepan and boil over high heat for several minutes to reduce and intensify the sauce.

Serve the ribs with the sauce passed separately.

"Buffalo has a bold flavor and is very lean, and very appealing to the healthy eater." —Frederick Clabaugh

Olson's High Country Bison (olsonshighcountrybison.com) sells grass-fed bison in Alberta and promotes the conservation, preservation, and restoration of the plains bison. This classic osso buco (Italian for "bone with a hole") is usually made with veal bones that are crosscut so you can get at the marrow. Bison is a natural substitute. Serve this with risotto, polenta, or mashed potatoes. Braised dishes always taste better the next day.

Olson's High Country Braised Bison Shanks

Makes 6 to 8 servings

In a large nonstick skillet or wide sauté pan over medium-high, heat the oil. Add the shanks, in batches, and brown on all sides, adding oil as needed. Set the shanks aside in a bowl.

Preheat the oven to 300°F.

In a large Dutch oven or ovenproof pot or roasting pan over medium-high heat, melt the butter. Add the celery, carrots, and onion. Cook, stirring, until the vegetables begin to brown, about 8 minutes. Add the garlic. Cook, stirring, for 2 minutes. Stir in the tomatoes with their juices, tomato paste, stock, rosemary, thyme, parsley, bay leaves, wine if using, salt, peppercorns, and cloves. Add the reserved shanks with their juices. If needed, add more water or stock to just cover the shanks.

Put the pan, uncovered, in the oven. Cook, stirring once or twice, until the meat is very tender, about 3 to 4 hours. Transfer the meat to a platter. Strain the braising liquid, discarding the solids.

If desired, place the braising liquid in a medium saucepan and boil over medium-high heat until reduced slightly.

Serve the shanks with the sauce passed separately.

1 Tbsp vegetable oil (preferably peanut or grapeseed)

5 to 6 lb bison shanks, cut crosswise into 2- to 3-inch-thick sections

2 Tbsp unsalted butter

2 stalks celery, diced

2 carrots, peeled and diced

1 medium yellow onion, diced

1 Tbsp minced garlic

1 (28 oz) can diced tomatoes

3 Tbsp tomato paste

6 cups stock (any combination of bison, beef, chicken, or vegetable)

1 sprig fresh rosemary

12 sprigs fresh thyme

8 sprigs flat-leaf parsley

2 bay leaves

1 cup dry red wine (optional)

1 tsp kosher salt

15 black peppercorns

4 whole cloves

Meeting Bailey Jr.

I'd read the stories and seen the YouTube videos. What I wanted to do was meet Bailey Jr., a world-famous pet bison, and maybe even watch him go for a spin in his customized convertible. It took some major wheedling, but I finally convinced Jim Sautner, Bailey Jr.'s human dad, to let me make the eight-hour drive north to Spruce Grove on the outskirts of Edmonton, Alberta.

Our bison are wild. We can't pat them. They live ordinary lives that don't intersect with CNN or Animal Planet. They haven't visited the local pub or the Calgary Stampede. They don't do parades.

But it wasn't the cult of celebrity that drew me to Bailey Jr.—it was simply the chance to tousle his soft, shaggy coat. I wanted to pat a bison something fierce. I imagined it would be like stroking one of our bison rugs, except with the living, breathing, and incredibly dangerous animal underneath it.

"I've turned down *National Geographic* and 30 or 40 other media requests," grouses Jim during last-minute negotiations on the big day. He's packing to move to a new acreage and wants to cancel. His wife, Linda, the lovely office manager for the Bison Producers of Alberta, can't get away from work. The skies are gray. A storm is coming.

But I'm just 90 minutes away, and the journalist in me won't take no for an answer. We negotiate a five-minute meeting in the field. I tell Rick to stay in the van with the kids.

"I got the car started," says Jim amiably when I arrive, his packing clearly put on hold. A burgundy Pontiac Parisienne waits in the driveway. He created this "Baileymobile" from a sedan, removing the windshield, windows, passenger seat, and backseats and cutting off the roof for a TV crew.

BAILEY JR., JIM SAUTNER, AND CHARLIE BROWN

"Have you got your camera ready?" Jim asks as we walk a few steps from the house to the field where Bailey Jr. stands by the fence. "Your first shots will be of him sucking on my hand."

As he and Bailey display their intense bond, Jim tells me his beloved bison is five years old, weighs almost 2,300 pounds (1,040 kg), and is still growing.

This unusual story starts in 2000, when Jim took in a bison calf that needed to be bottle-fed. He named him Bailey D. Buffalo and marveled at his docile temperament and the fact that he loved his human family more than his herd. When the *Edmonton Journal* photographed Bailey Sr. in the Sautners' living room, the story exploded. Bailey Sr. met royalty (Queen Elizabeth II), appeared in a couple of movies, learned to line-dance, and celebrated his fourth birthday at a fancy hotel with a bash attended by Alberta's then-premier Ralph Klein.

Bailey Sr. started earning impressive appearance fees, but died in a freak corral accident (he snagged his foot in a bale feeder) in 2008 when he was just eight years old. Bison usually live 20 to 25 years.

Just a few weeks later, a neighbor called the grief-stricken Jim about another orphaned calf. Jim and Linda didn't expect lightning to strike twice, but the bison (who was originally named Brady until "the media and marketing people said go with Bailey Jr.") also

BAILEY JR. AND JIM SAUTNER

grew up relatively docile and amenable to training. He has become an ambassador for Alberta's bison industry.

The Sautners' home, just off the busy Yellowhead Highway, is the second driveway on a service road. The property is marked by a wagon wheel and a sign for Sterling Ranches. Besides a cocker spaniel named Charlie Brown, Bailey Jr. is the only animal in sight. "The bank broke me. I had to get rid of them all," says Jim of his former bison herd.

If there's one thing I know about bison, it's that they're a herd animal and usually can't bear to be alone (except for some of the old bulls outside of breeding season). "I'm his herd, actually," Jim says of Bailey Jr. "When I come home every day, he'll run up to the end of the fence."

Wearing Wranglers and a white cowboy hat, Jim holds a shoehorn to tap the bison's horns if he misbehaves. "It tells him to keep his horns away from me, but not his face."

Bailey acts up from the get-go the day I visit, tossing his head and expressing what seems to be displeasure with the rope halter around his head.

"Hey, quit it," Jim growls. He explains that bison "get hard to handle" between the ages of three and five. He regales me with the story of how Bailey knocked him in the chest with both horns and caused a fairly serious injury during a break from a TV shoot.

Today's imminent storm seems to be putting all of us on edge. "When the wind comes up like this, it bothers all buffalo," explains Jim. "They don't like wind because they can't hear predators."

Even so, Bailey Jr. walks happily to "his" car and hops in without complaint. He's eager to get to the black plastic tub of oats strapped to the hood.

"I'll drive up the driveway for you," offers Jim. "They fined me 4,000 dollars for being out on this road with him."

This is more than I had hoped for. I gawk as Jim drives his beloved pet around the yard for almost an hour, stopping occasionally to share memories and anecdotes. His deep love for Bailey is clear. His affectionate grin for the animal lights up his face.

But still, we're talking about a massive wild animal with aggressive instincts that can kick with only a split second's notice. When we drive guests around our ranch for a "buffalo safari" and stop for pictures, we tell them to stick close to the truck and warn them that bison are dangerous and unpredictable.

"If you know how to handle them, they're not," insists Jim.

Bailey Jr. is not a young mom protecting her calf, and he's not a bull asserting his pecking order during mating season. But he's moody. One moment he's standing serenely in his car, the next he's angrily tossing his head. Jim blames himself. He has been putting in long hours doing oil-field work and hasn't been spending much time with Bailey. "Yeah, he used to be really good and he'll get better once I start working with him again."

Bailey rubs his head and horns against the car.

"When you get your new car, you can't do this," Jim warns him fondly, alluding to a Cadillac in Bailey's future.

Jim urges me to bring my family over for a few photos, which I do despite feeling uneasy. Soon after the kids are safely back in our van, Bailey Jr. announces he's had enough. He hops out of his convertible and head-butts the rear end of it.

"Hey, you son of a bitch, that's enough," shouts Jim. He gives Bailey Jr. an ample length of rope and steers him toward a patch of grass. On the way, the disgruntled bison head-butts another car, this time doing obvious damage.

"I knew I shouldn't have done this today," says an angry Jim. "He's not something I'm proud of today."

I leave unsettled. Patting Bailey Jr. was exactly as imagined. I witnessed a rare bond between man and animal, but feel no desire to have my own pet bison or even pat a bison again. The danger terrifies me.

Later, I look up Animal Planet's *Fatal Attractions* documentary series about people who risk life and limb to live with deadly pets. There's a two-minute clip online that shows Bailey Jr. ripping up the rug in the Sautners' living room and then riding placidly in his convertible.

"One of the things that I've always thought about death and dying is I don't want to die with my boots on," Jim tells the show. "I want to get run over by a big old buffalo while out in the pasture, and I mean that's the way I want to go."

CHAPTER 6

Sausages

Cook sausages to 160°F using a digital thermometer. Be sure the juices run clear when the sausages are pierced with the tip of a knife. Count on 15 to 25 minutes of cooking time no matter what cooking method you use.

Oven: Roast sausages, drizzled with olive oil, in a preheated cast-iron skillet in an oven heated to 400°F, turning once.

Stovetop: Put sausages in a skillet filled with 1 inch of water. Cover and cook on high heat for 10 minutes. Uncover and cook over medium-high heat, turning often and adding water as needed.

Barbecue: Grill sausages directly over medium-high heat, turning often.

I came to baked sausages late in life after years of greasy splatters while panfrying. What a revelation. Choose a mild sausage here since you're going to be smothering it with assertive toppings. There's a lot of room for personal choice. Do you like your buns big and crusty, or thin and unobtrusive? I like mine thin and multigrain. As for the beer, please experiment with local craft varieties.

Baked Bison Sausages with Drunken Toppings

Makes 4 hot dogs

In a large nonstick skillet over medium, heat 2 tablespoons of the olive oil. Add the onions and cook for 30 minutes, stirring occasionally. Stir in the mushrooms, bell peppers, and remaining 2 tablespoons of olive oil. Cook, stirring, for 30 minutes or until the onions are dark brown and caramelized. You may need to turn the heat down. Season to taste with black pepper. Stir in the beer and raise the heat to high. Cook, stirring often, until the beer is absorbed. Transfer the vegetables to a serving bowl. (If making ahead, refrigerate until ready to use and microwave to warm before serving.)

Preheat the oven to 400°F.

Place a medium cast-iron or ovenproof skillet in the oven for 5 minutes. Add the sausages to the skillet. Drizzle with the canola oil. Roast, turning once, until the sausages are cooked through and the juices run clear when the sausages are pierced with a knife, about 20 to 25 minutes.

Let the sausages stand for 5 minutes before serving in the buns topped with the beery onion mixture.

4 Tbsp extra-virgin olive oil, divided

2 large yellow onions, halved and thinly sliced

8 oz cremini mushrooms, thinly sliced

2 red, orange, or yellow bell peppers, thinly sliced

Freshly ground black pepper

1 (11½ oz) bottle dark beer (such as a stout or porter)

4 bison sausages (about 1 lb total)

1 Tbsp canola oil

4 buns, toasted or warmed if desired

Watercress is an underrated green. This peppery relative of mustard is rather easy to love. Obviously this dish takes on the personality of the sausages, so be sure to experiment. Enjoy this one-dish dinner as is, or pour it over steamed rice.

Bison Sausages with Wilted Watercress

Makes 4 servings

In a large saucepan or a large, deep skillet over medium-high heat, combine the sausages and 1 inch of water. Cook for 10 minutes, turning often, until the sausages are well browned and the water has evaporated. Cut each sausage on the diagonal into 4 pieces; set aside. Add the onion and oil to the skillet. Cook, stirring, for 6 minutes to soften. Add the tomatoes. Season to taste with salt and pepper. Cook, stirring, for 1 minute. Add the watercress, sausages, and water. Raise the heat to high and bring to a boil. Reduce the heat to low, cover, and simmer for 20 minutes, stirring occasionally and adding water if needed.

To serve, divide the sausages among 4 bowls. Top each with equal portions of the soupy watercress mixture.

1½ lb bison sausages (about 6)

1 large yellow onion, chopped

1 Tbsp canola oil

2 tomatoes, quartered

Kosher salt

Freshly ground black pepper

2 bunches watercress, washed and trimmed

2 cups water

Frittatas are an ideal way to transform breakfast into a quick dinner. If your sausages are mild, jack up the dried spices. If your sausages are bursting with flavor, consider leaving out the spices. Anything goes with the cheese. If you have any frittata left over, it makes a great sandwich filling. Of course, you can always make this for a weekend brunch.

Bison Sausage + Sweet Potato Frittata

Makes 6 servings

In a 9- or 10-inch cast-iron or ovenproof skillet over medium, heat the oil. Add the sausage meat. Cook, stirring often and using a wooden spoon to break up the meat, until the meat is browned, about 6 minutes. Add the onion, cumin, coriander, and ancho powder. Cook, stirring, for 6 minutes to soften the onion. Stir in the cilantro or parsley.

Meanwhile, preheat the broiler.

In a medium mixing bowl, whisk the eggs with the milk. Season to taste with salt and pepper. Stir in the sweet potato and the sausage mixture. Pour into the skillet, stirring to combine. Sprinkle with the cheese. Cook over medium heat until the eggs are set on the bottom but still runny on top, about 6 to 10 minutes.

Transfer the skillet to the oven and cook under the broiler until the eggs are set on top and the cheese is bubbling, about 3 to 5 minutes.

Serve hot or at room temperature.

1 Tbsp extra-virgin olive oil

8 oz bison sausages (about 2), casings removed

1 medium yellow onion, finely chopped

1 tsp ground cumin

1 tsp ground coriander

1 tsp ancho chili powder

¼ cup cilantro or flat-leaf parsley leaves, chopped

9 large eggs

½ cup milk

Kosher salt

Freshly ground black pepper

1 cup peeled, diced, and cooked sweet potato

½ cup grated or crumbled cheese, such as feta, chèvre, or aged white cheddar

I've been eating quinoa for about a decade and was thrilled when it suddenly caught fire in North America after languishing in the health food/bulk store realm. This supernutritious, grain-like seed makes a great change from rice. Here I use it to build an all-in-one meal that takes its main flavor from the type of sausage that you use. This dish works just as well cold as it does warm. Red and black quinoa take a couple more minutes to cook than white quinoa, but add extra flavor. I like to mix all three.

Quinoa with Bison Sausage + Veggie Medley

Makes 4 to 6 servings

In a medium saucepan over high heat, bring the water to a boil. Add the quinoa. Reduce the heat to low and cover. Simmer for 12 to 15 minutes until the grains are puffed. Drain any remaining water and return the quinoa to the pot. Cover and let stand for 5 minutes. Fluff with a fork. Transfer to a large mixing bowl.

Meanwhile, preheat the oven to 400°F.

Put a medium cast-iron or ovenproof skillet in the oven to heat for 5 minutes. Add the sausages. Bake for 20 minutes. Let stand for 5 minutes before slicing into rounds. Halve each round. Add the sausages with their juices to the quinoa.

At the same time, in a large nonstick skillet over medium-high, heat 1 tablespoon of the oil. Add the mushrooms. Cook, stirring, until the mushrooms release and reabsorb liquid, about 10 minutes. Stir into the quinoa mixture.

In the same skillet over medium-high, heat another 1 tablespoon of the oil. Add the red pepper, celery, onion, and garlic. Cook, stirring, until the vegetables soften, about 7 minutes. Add the broccoli. Cook, stirring, for 2 minutes. Stir the vegetables into the quinoa mixture.

In a small bowl, whisk together the remaining 3 tablespoons of oil, balsamic vinegar, and grainy mustard. Stir into the quinoa mixture. Mix well. Season to taste with salt and pepper.

3 cups water

1½ cups white, red, and/or black quinoa, rinsed

1 lb bison sausages (about 4)

5 Tbsp extra-virgin olive oil, divided

2 portobello mushrooms, stems discarded, caps chopped

1 red bell pepper, diced

2 stalks celery, diced

1 medium yellow onion, finely diced

4 cloves garlic, minced

1 cup small broccoli-florets

2 Tbsp balsamic vinegar

2 Tbsp grainy mustard

Kosher salt

Freshly ground black pepper

I like this simple scramble with maple sausages, but any flavor will work. Whether you eat this for breakfast, lunch, or dinner, it's a fast and satisfying meal.

Bison Sausage Scramble

Makes 2 servings

In a medium bowl, lightly beat the eggs with a whisk or fork. Stir in the cilantro or parsley. Season to taste with salt and pepper.

In a medium nonstick skillet over medium-high, heat the oil. Add the onion and bell pepper. Cook, stirring, for 5 minutes to soften. Add the sausage meat. Cook, stirring and breaking up the meat, until it is cooked through, about 8 minutes. Reduce the heat to medium. Add the egg-herb mixture. Cook, stirring gently with a wooden spoon, until just scrambled. Transfer the mixture to a plate.

If serving with tortillas, wipe out the skillet and heat over medium. Add the tortillas in two batches. Cook until warmed through, about 1 minute per side.

Serve the sausage scramble with the tortillas or toast on the side.

4 large eggs

¼ cup chopped cilantro or flat-leaf parsley

Kosher salt

Freshly ground black pepper

1 Tbsp extra-virgin olive oil

1 medium yellow onion, diced

½ red bell pepper, diced

8 oz bison sausages (about 2), casings removed

4 soft corn tortillas (each about 5 inches in diameter), or 4 slices buttered toast

The Swiss call this oversize potato pancake a rösti. The Jewish community makes a smaller version and calls it a latke. I'm calling it an oversize hash brown. If you're not up for the challenge of flipping this in and out of the skillet, you can always make pancake-size versions by using a ½-cup measure.

One Big Bison Hash Brown

Makes 4 to 6 servings

In a medium nonstick skillet (about 10 inches in diameter) over medium heat, cook the sausage meat for 6 minutes, using a wooden spoon to break up the meat into small pieces. Add the green onions. Cook, stirring, until the sausage is crisp, about 2 to 3 minutes. Transfer the mixture to a bowl. Stir in 2 tablespoons of the oil.

Using the large holes on a box grater, coarsely grate the potatoes into a large bowl. One handful at a time, squeeze the potatoes to release their liquid; discard the liquid. (You may want to do this twice.) Return the potatoes to the bowl. Stir in the sausage mixture. Sprinkle with salt and pepper to taste.

In the same skillet over medium-low, heat another 2 tablespoons of the oil. Add the potato-sausage mixture. Press with a spatula to firmly pack and make an even layer. Cover with a lid or foil. Cook for 10 minutes. Remove the lid or foil. Cook until the bottom is golden, about 5 minutes. Watch carefully and adjust the heat if needed. Use a spatula to loosen the sides and bottom of the hash brown.

Place a large dinner plate over the skillet. Carefully flip so the hash brown is on the plate.

In the skillet over medium-low, heat the remaining 2 tablespoons of oil. Slide the hash brown back into the skillet, with the browned side up. Cover with a lid or foil. Cook for 5 minutes. Uncover. Cook until the bottom is browned and the potatoes are cooked through, about 10 minutes. (Watch carefully and adjust the heat if needed.)

If needed, run the spatula around the sides and bottom again before sliding the hash brown onto a serving plate. Cut into 4 to 6 wedges.

8 oz bison sausages (about 2), casings removed

6 green onions, thinly sliced

6 Tbsp extra-virgin olive oil, divided

1½ lb russet potatoes, peeled if desired

Kosher salt

Freshly ground black pepper

Kale is a nutritional powerhouse that lends a much more subtle green presence to a casserole than assertive spinach. I love this with a feisty chorizo sausage. If you're using a mild sausage, throw in a bunch of dried spices or fresh herbs for flavor.

Cheesy Pasta Bake with Bison Sausage + Kale

Makes 6 to 8 servings

In a large saucepan filled with boiling water, cook the pasta according to the package instructions until al dente. Drain well.

Preheat the oven to 400°F.

In a large skillet over medium-high, heat the oil. Add the onion and garlic. Cook, stirring, for 5 minutes to soften. Add the bison meat. Cook, stirring and breaking up the meat with a wooden spoon, until it is cooked through, about 8 minutes. Add the kale. Cook, stirring, until wilted. Stir in the tomatoes with their juices and the cream.

Transfer the mixture to a large round casserole or a 13 × 9-inch baking dish. Sprinkle with the cheese. Bake until the cheese melts and the sauce bubbles, about 15 minutes.

1 lb short dried pasta (such as rotini, bow tie, or penne)

2 Tbsp extra-virgin olive oil

1 large yellow onion, chopped

3 cloves garlic, minced

1 lb bison chorizo or other sausage (about 4), casings removed

½ large bunch kale, trimmed and chopped

1 (28 oz) can crushed tomatoes

¼ cup whipping cream

2 cups grated mozzarella

Jill O'Brien spent her career catering and creating restaurants. Now she runs Wild Idea Buffalo Co. (wildideabuffalo.com) in Rapid City, South Dakota, with her rancher/writer husband, Dan O'Brien. The company ships its meat across the United States. This is one of Jill's creations—a sweet and intense Bolognese with the licorice kick of fennel. She uses mild, sweet bison breakfast sausage, but any kind of sausage would work.

Wild Idea Buffalo's Bison Bolognese

Makes 6 servings

In a large nonstick skillet over medium-high, heat the oil. Add the sausage meat, onion, garlic, oregano, basil, fennel seeds, rosemary, salt, and pepper. Cook, stirring, until the sausage is browned, 6 minutes. Stir in the wine. Add the tomatoes with their juices, water, brown sugar, lemon juice, and balsamic vinegar. Raise the heat to high and bring to a boil. Reduce the heat to low and simmer, uncovered, for 30 minutes or until desired thickness. (Makes about 4 to 5 cups.)

Meanwhile, in a large pot of boiling, salted water over high heat, cook the pasta according to the package instructions until al dente. Drain well.

Add the pasta to the simmering sauce in the skillet. Cook, tossing with tongs, until the pasta is coated with sauce.

Serve topped with cheese.

1 Tbsp extra-virgin olive oil

1 lb Italian bison sausage (such as breakfast, mild, or chorizo; about 4), casings removed, meat crumbled

1 medium yellow onion, diced

1 Tbsp minced garlic

1 Tbsp dried oregano leaves

1 Tbsp dried basil

2 tsp dried fennel seeds, crushed

1 tsp finely chopped fresh rosemary

1 tsp kosher salt

1 tsp freshly ground black pepper

½ cup red wine

1 (28 oz) can crushed tomatoes

1 cup water

1 Tbsp light brown sugar

1 Tbsp fresh lemon juice

1½ tsp balsamic vinegar

1 lb dried spaghetti or other pasta

Grated Parmesan cheese, to top

The Bison Whisperer

To be a "whisperer" is to have an extraordinary ability to read, understand, and communicate with an animal. It's a term that took off in the 1990s when Nicholas Evans wrote *The Horse Whisperer* and Robert Redford directed and starred in the movie version of the best-selling novel.

Horse and dog whisperers abound. Bison whisperers are much more rare. I've seen the label used to describe people like Albertan Jim Sautner and Texan RC Bridges, who've turned bison into pets. I've also heard it applied to Ivan Smith, who helps fellow ranchers cope with their animals.

Ivan, as luck would have it, is an Albertan. He runs Big Bend Bison Ranches near Penhold, as well as the Big Bend Market in Red Deer. The market is just five hours from our ranch, so Ivan and I agree to meet on a Monday morning after a long weekend at the Calgary Folk Festival.

Ivan comes by his nickname honestly, from years of hard work, but owes credit to his wife, Sharlyn Carter-Smith, for capitalizing on it. "I pitched Ivan as the bison whisperer and it took off," explains Sharlyn, a marketing expert who met her future husband while shopping in his store. "I really wanted to have more attention drawn to bison and the producers because nobody was hearing their stories."

Indeed, Ivan has been in the bison business since 1998, but only started grabbing media attention as a bison whisperer in 2012.

"'Bison Whisperer' in Demand across Southern Alberta," the *Calgary Herald* wrote on April 16 of that year.

"Expert Handler Displays Command over Bison," read a *Western Producer* headline on April 26.

CTV followed in June with "Bison Whisperer Helps Ranchers with Aloof Animals."

Ivan is just as advertised—quiet and soft-spoken. His calm demeanor clearly resonates with frustrated ranchers, unruly bison that have gotten loose, and stubborn bison that resist being rounded up and loaded onto trucks. He's also pretty young for a rancher—just 38 when we meet and already the vice-chair of the Bison Producers of Alberta. He keeps a base herd of 350 bison cows plus an ever-changing number of feeder bulls and calves.

Big Bend Market is a gleaming, 5,000-square-foot (450-square-meter) upscale meat market, deli, and gourmet food store. There's loads of beautiful bison meat—fresh rib steaks, T-bones, striploins, and short ribs, but also bison sausages, hot dogs, pepperoni, jerky, and bacon, and smoked buffalo. This foodie paradise boasts Maldon sea salt, juniper berries, fancy pasta, small-batch preserves, and local, artisan mustard. I order a Montreal-style smoked bison sandwich from the deli.

Ivan has come a long way since he bought his first bison and watched prices suddenly plummet. At times, he picked up other people's animals just to collect $130 a head from a government program. When a freak hailstorm caused his cows to "come up open" (not get pregnant), he convinced a supermarket chain to take them as burger. At one point, he sold at seven farmers' markets every week.

But the constant hustle and driving back and forth were exhausting, and soon a frustrated Ivan realized that a better way to sell a local, sustainable, quality product like bison was to create his own store. People said it wouldn't fly in a small city like Red Deer, but the store now has 26 employees and a second location mainly for production. Ivan supplies bison to hotels and restaurants, and has an interest in two restaurants. To keep up with demand, he must process more than 6,000 bison a year.

On top of all this, Ivan's the go-to man for people with bison trouble and bison for sale. It's no wonder that a man so immersed in bison has become a whisperer.

We're driving to his ranch when his cell phone starts ringing. "That guy has 10 finished bulls for sale," relays Ivan after a short conversation. "I hate Mondays in some ways because every bison farmer in the world calls."

IVAN SMITH, SHARLYN CARTER-SMITH, HAZEL, CHARLIE, AND RICK WITH SARAH

Got a skinny bison? One with a bum leg? Another with a bad eye? Maybe some mean old bulls? Call Ivan. "Everybody knows I like the big, scary ones."

There's even a mammoth bison looming on the side of his black Ford F-350 Super Duty truck. "I want a bison busting out of the side of my truck," Ivan told a graphic designer, who worked with pictures of three different animals to create the dramatic image.

Bison, Ivan says, can read people, just like he can "read" the animals' moods and predict which ones are going to chase him.

"It's beautiful, really," sighs Sharlyn. "They don't want to be aggressive."

We visit one herd that's grazing on seeded pasture. There are four large, dark wood bison in among the smaller and lighter-colored plains bison.

"You can smell it's breeding season," says Ivan. I don't smell anything, but I do hear coyote pups yipping nearby and see that this herd isn't thrilled to see us.

IVAN SMITH AND SHARLYN CARTER-SMITH

"Sometimes they come around, but right now I can see they want to escape," says Ivan. "They're ready to be moved off this grass."

One bison meanders over. "Hi, Sarah. Hi, beautiful," coos Sharlyn. "She's very friendly, this girl."

Sarah was bottle-fed by a previous owner but is still wild enough to live with the herd. "She knows that as long as I'm close, nobody will mess with her," explains Ivan. "She becomes like an alpha female because she's comfortable around people."

Sarah may be comfortable coming close to strangers, but she doesn't let me touch her. I'm glad there's some wild left in her.

I ask Ivan to share his bison-whispering tips. He tells me, "Look at how they carry themselves. Watch their body language. Listen to the noises they make. Know that they can smell fear. Never trust a fence."

Bison can run up to 30 miles per hour (50 kilometers/hour), reaching top speeds in just a few strides. They can turn on a dime and knock down fences.

Ivan has had two close calls, both while helping other ranchers.

In one incident, he had a bad feeling about a gate, and sure enough, a bison cow charged just as he chained it. He jumped back. The gate swung, ripped his coat open, hit the fence, and bounced back, knocking him on top of the now-dead cow. She killed herself crashing so forcefully into the gate.

At another farm with "a terrible setup" for handling bison, Ivan was in a pen when the farmer's neighbor stupidly whacked a bison's butt with a stock prod. The animal tossed Ivan in the air with its horns.

He lived. He learned.

"For the most part, bison really just want to get away," advises Ivan, "so you just use that to your advantage."

There's no call for any bison whispering today. We don't need to round them up, tag them, or load them onto a truck. We let them be.

CHAPTER 7

Odd Bits

I love the term "odd bits," coined by fellow Torontonian Jennifer McLagan in *Odd Bits: How to Cook the Rest of the Animal* (Ten Speed Press, 2011). It's a broader term than offal or variety meats—and it simply has a better ring to it.

If you're buying a whole bison, you can ask for the odd bits as part of the package. I've never been able to get my hands on the meaty cheeks, and I have to admit that I don't yet love the kidneys or sweetbreads. But I've come to love heart, tongue, liver, tail, testicles, and bones. I hope you'll give some of these a try. The bits are very difficult to get from stores, but if you order directly from a rancher, you should be able to get them.

White stock uses raw, rather than roasted, bones. I like it because it's quicker than making brown stock. Timothy Wasylko, Prime Minister Stephen Harper's personal chef at 24 Sussex Drive in Ottawa, Ontario, taught me how to make this stock.

White Bison Stock

Makes about 8 cups

In a large stockpot, combine the bones, cold water, onions, celery, carrot, parsley, thyme, bay leaves, and peppercorns. Bring to a boil over high heat. Skim off any scum that rises to the surface. Reduce the heat to about medium to maintain a slow simmer. Simmer for 4 to 6 hours, skimming any scum and adding a little water if you simmer too strongly and the liquid gets low. Strain, discarding the solids.

Refrigerate until cold. Scrape away the fat. Refrigerate, or freeze in small containers, until ready to use.

4½ lb bison bones (mix of marrow, knuckle, rib, shin, spine), rinsed

12 cups cold water

2 medium yellow onions, chopped

2 stalks celery, chopped

1 carrot, chopped

1 bunch flat-leaf parsley stems

1 bunch fresh thyme

2 bay leaves

4 black peppercorns

This takes just a little more work than the White Bison Stock (see opposite page), as you must roast the bones. But the payoff is a stronger, more intense flavor.

Brown Bison Stock

Makes about 16 cups

Preheat the oven to 400°F.

In a large roasting pan, spread out the bones. In a separate roasting pan, spread out the onions, celery, and carrots. Roast the bones and vegetables for 1 hour.

Transfer the bones and vegetables to a large stockpot. Add the cold water, tomato paste, parsley stems, thyme, bay leaves, and peppercorns. Bring to a boil over high heat. Skim off any scum that rises to the surface. Reduce heat to about medium to maintain a gentle simmer. Simmer for 4 to 6 hours, skimming any scum and adding water if you simmer too hard and the liquid gets low. Strain, discarding the solids.

Refrigerate until cold. Scrape away the fat. Refrigerate, or freeze in smaller containers, until ready to use.

6 to 7 lb bison bones (mix of marrow, knuckle, rib, shin, spine)

2 medium yellow onions, chopped

2 stalks celery, chopped

2 carrots, chopped

24 cups cold water

1 (5½ oz) can tomato paste

1 bunch flat-leaf parsley stems

1 bunch fresh thyme

3 bay leaves

1 tsp black peppercorns

Liver is a delight when it's cooked with a light touch so that it remains pink and tender. I don't know why people still soak liver in milk. If the animal is young enough, it should have a mild, pleasing flavor. A little liver goes a long way. Ditto cream. I like to eat this rich dish with a simple green salad. Bison liver cooks quickly, but be patient with the sauce. I learned to love liver at Batifole restaurant in Toronto (batifole.ca), and to cook it properly from a recipe by New York chef Daniel Boulud.

Panfried Bison Liver with Dijon-Shallot Cream Sauce

Makes 4 servings

Put the flour on a plate or in a shallow bowl. Stir in the salt and pepper. Add the liver and toss each piece to coat, shaking off the excess flour.

In a large nonstick skillet over medium, heat the oil. Add the liver. Cook for 2 minutes per side or until just cooked through but still pink in the center. Transfer to a plate and cover loosely with foil.

Add the butter to the skillet. Melt over medium heat. Add the shallots. Cook, stirring, for 5 minutes to soften. Add the red wine vinegar. Cook for 3 minutes or until nearly evaporated. Add the white wine. Cook, stirring occasionally, for 5 minutes or until the liquid is nearly evaporated. Stir in the cream. Simmer for 6 minutes. Stir in the grainy mustard. Transfer the sauce to a gravy boat.

Serve the liver with the sauce passed separately.

½ cup all-purpose flour

½ tsp kosher salt

¼ tsp freshly ground black pepper

1 lb bison liver, rinsed, patted dry, and cut into ½-inch strips (about 8)

2 Tbsp canola oil

2 Tbsp unsalted butter

2 large shallots, minced

2 Tbsp red wine vinegar

½ cup dry white wine, such as chardonnay

½ cup whipping cream

2 Tbsp grainy Dijon mustard

Jill O'Brien helps her rancher/writer husband, Dan, run the Wild Idea Buffalo Co. in Rapid City, South Dakota, shipping bison meat across the country from wildideabuffalo.com. After a career in catering and restaurants, Jill is often found in her test kitchen and is working on a cookbook. She uses Wild Idea's mild and sweet breakfast sausage for this pâté, but says you can use any kind of sausage, including chorizo for a spicy kick. If you don't have cognac or brandy, use bourbon or whisky.

Wild Idea Buffalo's Bison Liver Pâté

Makes about 1¼ cups

In a large nonstick skillet over medium-high heat, melt the butter. Add the liver, sausage meat, onion, garlic, pepper, salt, thyme, sage, nutmeg, and allspice. Cook, stirring, for 6 minutes. Add the cognac or brandy. Cook, stirring, for 2 minutes.

Transfer to a food processor. Add the paprika. Purée until smooth. Taste; adjust the seasoning if desired, pulsing to incorporate.

Line the inside of a bowl or mold with plastic wrap. Fill with the pâté, packing it tightly and smoothing the top. Cover with the plastic wrap and refrigerate overnight.

When you're ready to serve, remove the pâté from the mold and place it on a serving plate. Let it stand at room temperature for 1 hour. Serve with baguette slices, crackers, and/or apple slices, if desired.

¼ cup unsalted butter

8 oz bison liver, sliced and patted dry

4 oz bison sausage (about 1), casings removed

¼ medium yellow onion, chopped

2 tsp minced garlic

1 tsp freshly ground black pepper

½ tsp kosher salt

¼ tsp dried thyme

¼ tsp ground sage

Large pinch ground nutmeg

Pinch ground allspice

¼ cup cognac or brandy

½ tsp smoked paprika

OPTIONAL ACCOMPANIMENTS:
Baguette slices
Crackers
Apple slices

There's no middle ground with heart: cook it fast or slow. This smoked bison heart steak falls in the "fast" camp and comes from CHARCUT Roast House chef/owner Connie DeSousa and her co-chef John Jackson. Connie was living in San Francisco when she first tried heart at a Peruvian rotisserie and was blown away by the flavor and texture of what instantly became her new favorite steak. Her customers love it. At the Calgary restaurant (charcut.com), these heart steaks are paired with mustard-pickled onions and warm pretzel bread sticks. I've included a pickles recipe, but you can buy soft bread-sticks or an artisan loaf. The restaurant sometimes serves heart with its herb-packed chimichurri sauce.

CHARCUT Roast House's Bison Heart with Quick Pickles

Makes 4 servings

Soak the wood chips in a bowl of water for at least 1 hour. Drain. Place on a piece of foil, folding the sides over to create a packet but leaving a 3-inch opening at the top. Preheat your barbecue to medium-high. When it's hot, place the foil packet on the grill and close the lid. Heat until the chips are really smoking.

Place the heart steaks on a plate. Season with the oil, salt, and pepper.

Barbecue the heart steaks, uncovered, for 2 minutes per side. Move them to the upper rack and close the lid. Turn the heat to low. Smoke to desired doneness, about 10 minutes for medium-rare.

Serve the bison heart steaks with quick pickles or chimichurri, if desired.

1 cup fruit wood chips

1½ lb portion bison heart (about ½ of the heart), cut into 4 "steaks," trimmed, rinsed, and patted dry

1 Tbsp extra-virgin olive oil

½ tsp kosher salt

¼ tsp cracked black pepper

CHARCUT Roast House's Quick Pickles (optional, see opposite page)

Chimichurri Sauce (optional, see p. 86)

These tart pickles from CHARCUT Roast House work in harmony with the wood-smoked bison heart. The restaurant adores (and sells) "Prairie-grown, Prairie-made" Brassica mustard. If you don't live in Alberta, where it's sold in lots of gourmet food stores, you can buy it online from brassicamustard.com.

CHARCUT Roast House's Quick Pickles

Makes 4 servings

Place the cucumbers in a glass bowl. Add the onion.

In a small saucepan, combine the vinegar, water, pickling spice, grainy mustard, salt, and sugar. Bring to a boil over high heat. Remove from the heat. Let cool for 10 minutes. Pour over the cucumbers and onion. Refrigerate, covered, overnight.

To serve, drain well or remove the cucumbers and onion from the liquid as needed.

2 pickling cucumbers (each about 3 to 4 inches long), cut into ½-inch rounds

1 medium yellow onion, halved and thinly sliced

1 cup white vinegar

½ cup water

1 Tbsp pickling spice, wrapped in a cheesecloth sachet

3 Tbsp grainy mustard

2 tsp kosher salt

2 tsp granulated sugar

" Bison is something we grew up on in the Prairies, along with elk, deer, and moose. It has a wonderful flavor similar to the highest quality grass-fed beef, but also has so many other health advantages. To me, bison is 'taste of place' and will remain an ongoing feature both in our homes and at CHARCUT." —John Jackson

Here's a slow-cooked heart stew that's a fabulous way to experience the organ. The recipe comes from Bob Jackson and Susan Chin, who run Tall Grass Bison (tallgrassbison.com) in Promise City, Iowa. They got the recipe years ago from one of their customers. Their "truly free-range" herd lives in natural family groups and is 100 percent grass-fed on tall grass.

Tall Grass Bison's Bison Heart + Root Vegetables in Wine Sauce

Makes 6 to 8 servings

Cut the heart into ½-inch slices. Trim the fat and discard the arteries and veins. Pat dry. Generously season the slices with salt and pepper. Pour the flour into a shallow bowl. Dredge the slices in the flour, shaking off the excess.

In a large saucepan over medium-high heat, melt the butter. Add the heart slices in a single layer, in batches if needed. Cook for 1 minute per side to brown. Add the onion, carrots, potatoes, thyme, stock or water, and wine. Bring to a boil and then reduce the heat to low and cover. Simmer for 1 hour or until the heart is tender. Remove the thyme stalks.

Serve in large, shallow bowls.

1 whole bison heart (about 3½ lb), rinsed

Kosher salt

Freshly ground black pepper

¼ cup all-purpose flour

3 Tbsp unsalted butter

1 large yellow onion, chopped

2 large carrots, peeled and chopped

2 potatoes, peeled, if desired, and chopped

10 sprigs fresh thyme

1 cup bison or beef stock or water

1 cup dry red wine

Normally the femurs (the upper front leg bones, which aren't meaty enough to sell as shanks for osso buco) are trimmed for ground or sausage meat and then discarded. It's a shame because inside lurks marrow, a delicacy that is unspeakably luxurious and delicious. You'll need a butcher to prepare these bones for you with an electric saw. The marrow-bone part of the recipe is my own. The salad comes from Vancouver chef Chris Whittaker of Forage (foragevancouver.com). For the photo, it was served on a pretty bed of coarse sea salt.

Broiled Bison Marrow Bones with Parsley Salad

Makes 2 to 4 servings

If you are serving the bones to guests and want them to look pretty, draw the blood out by soaking the bones in cold water to cover mixed with 2 tablespoons of kosher salt in the fridge for up to 24 hours, changing the water and salt several times. Rinse the bones and pat them dry. Let them dry at room temperature for 1 hour. If you're fine with the rustic look, there's no need to soak the bones.

Preheat the broiler on high.

Place the bones, cut sides down, on a baking sheet. Broil for 6 minutes. Flip and broil for 4 minutes or until the marrow is hot, soft, and golden but not liquefied.

Transfer the bones to 2 to 4 serving plates. Sprinkle to taste with the flaky sea salt and paprika. Serve with small spoons and a knife. To eat, scoop out the marrow and spread it on slices of baguette.

Alternately, if making the salad, salt the marrow bones once they come out of the oven, but don't add the smoked paprika.

For the salad, in a bowl combine the parsley, oil, red wine vinegar, sea salt, and pepper. Toss well.

To serve, place a pile of parsley salad on each plate, alongside the bones and a few baguette slices.

2 bison femurs, knobs discarded, bones halved lengthwise (makes 4 pieces)

Flaky sea salt

Smoked paprika

Sliced baguette

PARSLEY SALAD (OPTIONAL):
Leaves from 1 bunch flat-leaf parsley, washed

2 Tbsp extra-virgin olive oil

1 Tbsp red wine vinegar

Pinch fine sea salt

Pinch freshly ground black pepper

In Vancouver, chef Chris Whittaker runs Forage, a farm-to-table/locavore restaurant (foragevancouver.com). Instead of toasting his homemade croutons with olive oil, garlic, and herbs, he mixes them with bison marrow. The chef, of course, has a creative way to finish the dish. He mixes peppercress and frisée with herb dressing, grills garlic scapes, poaches an egg (sous vide–style), and sprinkles the dish with "mushroom soil" (a mix of ground dried porcinis, dried morels, and hazelnuts). I've scaled that down here. If you have garlic scapes, feel free to add them in.

Forage Restaurant's Bison Bone Marrow Croutons with Salad

Makes 4 servings

Preheat the oven to 375°F.

To make rendered bison marrow, place the bones, marrow sides down, on a baking rack with a baking tray beneath. Cook for 1 hour. If the marrow is still in the bones, loosen with a paring knife. Allow to cool slightly. Strain the marrow from the tray into a glass container. Makes about ½ cup. Refrigerate the marrow until you are ready to use it. Discard the bones or reserve for Brown Bison Stock (p. 201).

For the croutons, in a large nonstick skillet over medium-high, heat the bison marrow until hot and melted. Add the bread. Turn with tongs until all sides are golden brown but not too crispy. Remove with a slotted spoon to a paper towel–lined bowl. Season to taste with salt and pepper.

For the salad, in a small bowl, whisk the oil and red wine vinegar until emulsified. Place the greens in a large bowl. Pour the vinaigrette over the greens. Toss well.

To serve, divide the salad over 4 plates. Top each with warm croutons and 1 poached egg, if using.

3 lb bison femurs, knobs discarded, bones halved lengthwise, to make rendered marrow

CROUTONS:
5 slices sourdough bread, torn into bite-size pieces (about 4 cups)
Fine sea salt
Freshly ground black pepper

SALAD:
3 Tbsp extra-virgin olive oil
1 Tbsp red wine vinegar
8 cups baby arugula or other mixed greens
4 poached eggs (optional)

Oxtails (skinned beef cattle tails) are beloved in parts of Asia, the Caribbean, and the American South. They haven't caught on with the North American mainstream, but that's a shame since they're cheap and deeply delicious. We hate to see any part of our bison go to waste, so we experiment with the tails even though they're not as meaty as those from cows. They're also hard to come by unless you're buying from a rancher, so feel free to substitute short ribs for the tail in this ode to Chinese flavors inspired by American cookbook author Cecilia Chiang.

Chinese-Style Bison Tails

Makes 2 to 4 servings

Place the tail pieces in a medium saucepan, and cover with water by 1 inch. Bring to a boil over high heat. Cook for 5 minutes. Drain, rinsing with cold water. Return the tails to the pan. Add the ginger and celery. Cover with cold water. Bring to a boil over high heat. Reduce the heat to low and cover. Simmer for 3 hours, stirring occasionally. Stir in the soy sauce, mushroom soy sauce, rice wine, and carrots. Raise the heat to high and bring to a boil. Reduce the heat to low, cover, and simmer for 30 minutes or until the carrots are tender-crisp. Stir in the sugar.

To serve, strain the mixture. Discard the ginger. Place the bison tails and vegetables in a serving bowl. Pass the soy braising liquid separately.

2 bison tails (about 2 lb), cut between the joints

2 thin slices fresh ginger

2 stalks celery, finely chopped

¼ cup soy sauce

2 Tbsp mushroom soy sauce

1 Tbsp Shaoxing rice cooking wine

3 carrots, peeled and finely chopped

2 tsp granulated sugar

Ideas for Tail

Bison tails are perfect in any slow-simmered soup or stew. Serve them as is to people who aren't shy about picking the meat from the bones. Otherwise pull the cooked meat from the bones yourself and add it to things like pasta sauce, hash, dumplings, perogies, and sandwiches.

Montreal's Au Pied de Cochon (restaurantaupieddecochon.ca) is famous for its decadent pork dishes, but it's this tongue dish that I love. There's a recipe for it in *Au Pied de Cochon: The Album* (Douglas & McIntyre, 2008), but it's made with venison and doesn't taste as sublime as I remember. I combined the written recipe with the notes I took while dining at the counter and watching the chefs in the open kitchen make the tongue. Then I simplified the dish, skipping the brining for a start. The result is so good it'll make a tongue lover out of anybody.

Pan-Seared Bison Tongue with Tarragon Sauce

Makes 4 servings

For the tongue, place it in a large saucepan and cover it with water. Add the onion, bay leaves, peppercorns, and salt. Bring to a boil over high heat. Reduce the heat to medium and cover. Simmer until the tongue is tender when pierced at the thickest part and the tip, and the skin peels off easily, about 3 to 4 hours, depending on the size.

Transfer the tongue to a cutting board. When it's cool enough to handle but still warm, peel away and discard the tongue's skin and any visible fat or gristle. Slice the tongue meat lengthwise as thinly as possible. Reserve ½ pound of tongue meat (enough meat for 4 servings) for this recipe. Refrigerate the remaining tongue slices for another use.

For the sauce, in a small bowl, stir together the red wine vinegar, grainy mustard, and tarragon leaves. Whisk in the oil. Season to taste with salt. Refrigerate until ready to use. (Makes about 1 cup.)

For the vegetables, bring a medium saucepan of water to boil over high heat. Add the carrots. Cook for 2 minutes to soften. Drain well.

Dry out the saucepan. Heat the oil over medium. Add the carrots and onion. Cook, stirring, until lightly browned, about 8 minutes. Stir in the pickles and stock. Raise the heat to high and bring to a simmer, and then reduce the heat to low and keep warm.

BISON TONGUE:

1 bison tongue

1 medium yellow onion, quartered

3 bay leaves

2 Tbsp black peppercorns

1 tsp kosher salt

2 Tbsp unsalted butter

TARRAGON SAUCE:

2 Tbsp red wine vinegar

2 Tbsp grainy mustard

Chopped leaves from 1 bunch fresh tarragon

½ cup canola oil

Kosher salt

VEGETABLES:

4 carrots, peeled and finely diced

2 Tbsp extra-virgin olive oil

1 medium yellow onion, finely diced

2 dill pickles, finely diced

2 cups bison or beef stock

To serve the tongue, heat a large nonstick skillet over medium-high. Add the butter. When it melts, add the reserved tongue slices in a single layer. Cook until browned, about 1 to 2 minutes per side if the tongues are warm, 3 to 4 minutes per side if they're cold.

Add the vegetable-stock mixture to the skillet. Boil for 1 minute. Remove from the heat.

Arrange the tongue pieces on plates. Top with the vegetable-stock mixture and a dollop of the tarragon sauce.

Ideas for Tongue

Once you've poached and peeled your tongue, it's ready to be eaten cold or hot. Try the leftovers from this dish thinly sliced and smothered in just about any sauce. Chop or slice the tongue meat and eat it in Mexican tacos. Or thinly slice it and pile it on a sandwich.

Testicles are fun to serve and have a surprisingly mild flavor once you get beyond any squeamishness. Every summer, Bottlescrew Bill's Pub in Calgary, Alberta, runs a testicle festival. (See page 217 to read more about it.) Sous chef Paul Turgeon showed me how to make this perennial favorite: testicle-stuffed bison meatballs in fiery ancho-tomato sauce. "You should hear the people chanting 'Go! Go! Go! Eat your ball of fire,'" Paul says. Even if you can't bear the thought of eating testicles or you can't find them, don't skip this recipe. Make the meatballs (without the testicle centers) and the sauce to go with spaghetti.

Great Bison Balls of Fire

Makes 16 meatballs (for 4 main or 8 appetizer servings)

Place the bison testicles, bay leaf, and peppercorns in a large saucepan of water. Bring to a boil over high heat. Reduce the heat to medium. Simmer for 30 minutes. Drain. Put the testicles in an ice bath. When they are cold, peel off the outer layer of skin and discard it. Slice the testicles into thin medallions (each about ¼ inch thick). Reserve 16 medallions for this recipe, and save any remaining pieces for another use. Refrigerate until ready to use.

For the sauce, soak the anchos in a small bowl of boiling water for 15 minutes. Discard the stems and seeds. Roughly chop the anchos.

In a large saucepan over medium-high, heat the oil. Add the onion and garlic. Cook, stirring, for 5 minutes to soften. Add the anchos and soaking liquid, tomato paste, basil, oregano, and thyme. Cook, stirring, for 2 minutes. Add the wine. Cook, stirring, until the wine is almost evaporated. Add the tomatoes with their juices and the water. Bring to a boil over high heat. Reduce the heat to low. If time allows, simmer for 2 to 3 hours to let the flavors combine. Using an immersion blender, purée the sauce until smooth. Alternately, purée in a food processor or blender in batches. (Makes about 5 cups.)

TESTICLES:
2 bison testicles (each about 8 oz)
1 bay leaf
1 tsp black peppercorns

ANCHO SAUCE:
3 dried ancho chilies
2 Tbsp extra-virgin olive oil
1 medium yellow onion, chopped
3 cloves garlic, chopped
3 Tbsp tomato paste
1 tsp dried basil
1 tsp dried oregano leaves
1 tsp dried thyme
1 cup red wine
1 (28 oz) can whole or diced tomatoes
2 cups water

For the meatballs, preheat the oven to 375°F. Grease a baking sheet.

In a large mixing bowl, combine the bison, fresh chilies, egg, cayenne pepper, chili powder, Cajun spice, black pepper, paprika, and salt to taste. Mix well by hand. Divide into 16 balls.

Wrap each meatball around a testicle slice. Roll until smooth. Don't leave any cracks. Place the meatballs on the baking sheet. Bake until cooked through and browned, about 20 minutes.

Serve the meatballs drizzled with the sauce. Refrigerate any remaining sauce for another use.

BISON MEATBALLS:

2 lb ground bison

4 fresh red or green Thai chilies, or 1 large jalapeno, minced with seeds

1 large egg

1½ tsp cayenne pepper

1 tsp chili powder

1 tsp Cajun spice blend

1 tsp freshly ground black pepper

½ tsp paprika

Kosher salt

Ideas for Testicles

Once the testicles are cooked, peeled, and sliced, they are a culinary blank slate. Most people bread and fry them and serve them with a dipping sauce. Consider a beer batter, or dip them in flour, then egg, then dried bread crumbs or cornmeal. I find it easier to cook testicles and then peel them. Others swear by peeling them when they're partially frozen and then cooking them. When I try that, I usually nick the balls and they seep out and deflate when cooked.

OLIVIA (LEFT) AND MARESSA MALLEY (RIGHT)

SLICED BISON TESTICLES

PAUL TURGEON

You Need Balls for This Festival

There's a restaurant in Calgary, Alberta, that has a ball with balls. Bottlescrew Bill's Pub (which also houses Buzzards Restaurant & Bar) has been running an annual testicle festival since 1992 to showcase balls, which are known in polite circles as prairie oysters or Rocky Mountain oysters.

I dropped by for the 20th anniversary celebration in 2013 to eat the three all-time most popular appetizer dishes, which were offered for $9.99 a pop. There was Great Balls of Fire, bison meatballs stuffed with you-know-what in a fiery ancho-tomato sauce. Mixed Nuts featured testicle medallions sautéed with wine, herbs, and crushed walnuts in a rum-butter sauce. Finally, Battered Balls offered cornmeal battered testicle slices served with apple-raspberry chutney.

"I thought the phrase 'testicle festival' was an amusing one, but the reality is that people do eat the testicles," explains owner Stuart Allan. When ranchers brand their cattle, they castrate the male calves and feast on the balls. "We thought we would re-create this and make it a soft adventure and people could enjoy them in the safety and comfort of our restaurants—and have them prepared by a professional chef so they're well done and well disguised."

The festival starts in mid-June and ends in July during the Calgary Stampede when the testicles run out. The restaurant stocks up on as many balls as it can from multiple sources. Most of the balls come from young male cow calves, but some come from slightly older bison (which are never castrated, by the way).

"I've been here for years and it's lots of fun," says sous chef Paul Turgeon. "Personally I would probably never order them [balls] because, being a guy, it just doesn't seem right."

Paul usually sells about 90 orders of balls per festival, but in 2013 he sold out, restocked, and then sold out again, selling a record 180 orders. Staff even had to cut off one table—a corporate party that was eating more than its fair share of balls.

Luckily, the chef saves me the very last slices of poached balls so he can show me how to make each of the three dishes. I share the spoils with Maressa and Olivia Malley, who are servers at the restaurant and happen to be sisters.

"Some people are really freaked out by the idea," admits Maressa. "But everybody that had them really enjoyed them. Nobody thought they were gross or couldn't eat them."

Nobody, that is, except her kid sister Olivia. She struggles through a taste of meatball ("It doesn't taste bad—it's just gross") and a bite of cornmeal ball ("Don't cut them, that's what weirds me out"). But Olivia loses it with her smidgeon of dessert ball—which has a surprisingly strong and unfamiliar flavor—and rushes to the bathroom to spit out her mouthful.

Macho posturing aside, testicles are pretty mild. But they sure are fun to eat and a hoot to talk about.

Here's another creative take on prairie oysters from Bottlescrew Bill's Pub/Buzzards Restaurant & Bar in Calgary (bottlescrewbill.com), home of the annual testicle festival. Sous chef Paul Turgeon uses gooseberries, which can be hard to find, so I subbed in blueberries.

Bison Dessert Balls

Makes 4 servings

Place the testicle, bay leaf, and peppercorns in a medium sauce-pan of water. Bring to a boil over high heat. Reduce the heat to medium. Simmer for 30 minutes. Drain. Put the testicle in an ice bath until cold. Peel away the outer skin with a sharp paring knife and discard. Slice the testicle into 8 to 12 thin medallions. If not cooking immediately, refrigerate until ready to use.

In a medium nonstick skillet over medium-high, heat the oil. Add the testicle slices. Cook for 1 minute per side to brown and warm if needed. Add the shallot. Cook, stirring, for 2 minutes. Add the strawberries and wine. Season to taste with salt and pepper. Add the blueberries and walnut pieces. Cook for 1 minute. Remove from the heat. Add the rum, butter, and Demerara sugar, swirling and stirring until the mixture is sauce-like.

To serve, divide the testicles among 4 dessert plates. Spoon equal portions of nuts, berries, and sauce over each plate.

1 bison testicle (about 8 oz)
1 bay leaf
1 Tbsp black peppercorns
1 tsp extra-virgin olive oil
1 shallot, minced
2 strawberries, quartered
¼ cup white wine
Kosher salt
Freshly ground black pepper
12 blueberries
2 Tbsp walnut pieces
¼ cup dark rum
2 Tbsp unsalted butter, at room temperature
2 Tbsp Demerara sugar

" Testicles aren't as strong as liver, so I find they're similar to sweetbreads, which I like." —Paul Turgeon

Space Jerky

I'm deep in a northern Saskatchewan boreal forest snacking on space jerky with a couple of bison ranchers. It sounds wacky, but it's true.

Okay, technically the label says Trails End Buffalo Stix: Cranberry Craze (not jerky), but this soft and moist smoked bison and cranberry "meat snack" really did win a Snacks for Space contest and a spot on the International Space Station with Canadian astronaut Chris Hadfield. There's a YouTube video to prove it. It's called "Chris Hadfield and Some Incredibly [*sic*] Floating Canadian Space Food." In it, the celebrity astronaut known for videos and Tweets unpacks a bag of Canadian snacks that includes maple cookies, maple syrup, chocolate, smoked salmon pâté, and blueberry granola bars. "And, if I'm not too far away from you guys from Saskatchewan, I have some buffalo jerky right here—cranberry-flavored buffalo jerky," Chris enthuses as the package floats beside him.

The Canadian Space Agency invited people to nominate their favorite regional foods for the contest, and picked 12 space-worthy winners from 150 entries. "Jeff from Edmonton" nominated Buffalo Stix. The winning snacks all had long shelf lives, didn't produce many crumbs, and could be easily eaten in orbit.

Astronauts are just like earthlings when it comes to food. They eat three meals a day plus one or two snacks. "We have lots of food—it keeps us healthy," Chris says in his video. "It tastes good and also it's a really important social time of the day when you can get together, talk about what everybody's doing, and relax and really try and share the human part of being in space. Food's good up here."

It's also good down here on Earth at Judy and Kevin Wilkinson's bison farm near

Livelong, Saskatchewan. We're eating chopped Buffalo Stix on crackers spread with cream cheese and jalapeno jelly.

"We always wanted to create something that would be healthy and good and not have a lot of crap in it," explains Judy. "We wanted a pemmican product, something with fruit. There's tons of jerky out there, but it's tough and made from full muscle. We wanted something soft and easy to chew."

Pemmican is an Aboriginal creation of dried meat (usually bison, elk, or deer) that is pounded into a coarse powder and mixed with melted fat and berries. It became a staple for Canadian fur traders since it was nutritious and traveled well in prerefrigeration times. Jerky is lean meat that has been cut into strips, and then mixed with a spice rub or liquid marinade, cured, and dried or smoked. Meat sticks are a softer, easier-to-chew version of dried meat.

Judy worked with food scientists at the Saskatchewan Food Industry Development Centre (Food Centre) in Saskatoon in 2004 to develop a nutritious snack, ultimately choosing cranberries over blueberries. There's no MSG, wheat, soy, or filler in the protein-rich snack made with brown sugar and smoked with hickory. A 20-gram piece has 45 calories and just 0.4 grams of fat.

"We eat a lot of tenderloin," the Wilkinsons say, "and the rest of the meat goes to jerky."

The couple got into the bison business earlier than most. They moved to the Livelong area in 1977 with two friends and a school bus, during their "back-to-the-land" days. A year later, they bought their first bison and now keep about 100 cows, selling most of the offspring to others for finishing.

They named their 1,600-acre (650-hectare) farm Trails End Bison, because it feels like the end of the road. It's in a forest tucked between Crown land, a First Nation reserve, and Turtle Lake, where there have been multiple sightings of a mysterious monster. Some say it's a prehistoric beast. Others swear it's a mammoth sturgeon. Whatever it is, it doesn't bother the bison.

We drive by the lake to see part of the herd. They ignore us. We drive to another wooded area looking for the rest of the herd and don't find them. There's lots of dense forest for them to disappear into.

For years, Judy and Kevin lived a subsistence lifestyle, raising two sons, milking cows,

JUDY AND KEVIN WILKINSON

raising rabbits for meat. They cleared some of the land, and built fences, vegetable gardens, and a home.

Kevin indulged his passion for "oddball" cars, collecting upward of 400 of them "here, there, and everywhere." They're lined up in barns and sheds, under shelters and out in the open near the house. "I'm pretty eclectic," says Kevin, rhyming off some of his finds: 1947 Hudson, 1956 Lincoln, 1934 Terraplane, 1947 Oldsmobile, 1954 Nash, 1939 Plymouth, 1932 Buick, and 1946 DeSoto.

He had his fun collecting and reluctantly admits he should probably sell "a bunch of them" and use the money to fix up the others. But in the meantime, he's building a replica general store and a gas station. "I think I would've been quite happy to live 100 years ago. I like history and old things better than new things."

In fact, Kevin would love to step back 150 or 200 years and see the West when it was packed with millions of wild bison. Judy, meanwhile, is the family gardener and jerky boss. She is also a mediator and marriage commissioner on the side.

The jerky business is booming, thanks in part to the boost from space and despite the fact that Trails End does very little retail business, selling instead to schools, online, and at about 20 trade and craft shows across Alberta, Saskatchewan, and Manitoba. The company goes through about 7,000 pounds (3,000 kilograms) of meat each year to create jerky.

To sell within Saskatchewan, Judy creates jerky at the provincially licensed Drake Meats using meat from her herd. To sell to the rest of Canada, she uses the federally licensed Food Centre and buys chuck tenders or tri-tips from bison that have been slaughtered at a federal facility. The label and packaging changes, but the product doesn't. There is just one flavor.

Doing the shows is an enormous amount of work and travel, but Judy thrives on connecting with customers. She accepts checks and even just the promise of payment. She has left shows with customers owing her up to $800, and has never been stiffed. Judy urges me to read a letter posted on the fridge. "Thank you very much for making this jerky. It is very, very good," it reads. "I am enclosing the $40.00."

"I tell people that I'm trying to change the world to a more honest economy one stick of jerky at a time," says a satisfied Judy.

The jerky sells for an average of $1.50 a stick. The provincial line sells in bulk by the piece without labels. Twenty-five sticks cost $40 (that's $1.60 each), but 150 cost $175 (or $1.17 each). The federal line sells by the case with three sizes of packages. A case of twenty-five 20-gram packages costs $45, or $1.80 a piece. That drops to $1.50 a piece if you buy a package of 325. Shipping is about $10.

"I have a thing about the fact that good food is very expensive and poor food is cheap," admits Judy. "It really bothers me that we only create food for the wealthy people. I know it's expensive."

"We're trying to produce premium jerky," Kevin reminds her. "We're trying to develop a different kind of jerky that's more appealing."

"I've come to realize that I can't feed the whole world," continues Judy. "I can't create an unlimited supply of jerky, but there are enough people that can afford our jerky that absolutely love it."

As we munch on the jerky canapés, we talk about how the meat treat can be chopped, panfried, and used like bacon bits in soups and salads. It can be added to pasta sauce or scrambled into eggs. It can, of course, be eaten straight from the package without any fuss.

For lunch we feast on garden salad, roasted broccoli, and skewers of slow-cooked bison marinated with ginger, garlic, rice wine vinegar, and sambal oelek (an Asian chili sauce). "This would be tenderloin from either an old bull or an old cow," Kevin reveals. It does have a noticeably stronger flavor than our bison, which are not even two years old when they're slaughtered.

"See, we like that old flavor," chimes in Judy.

Old and new. Past and present. Earth and space. I love how this story combines two earthy ranchers living in a remote part of Canada with an ultramodern, social-media-savvy astronaut in a remote part of the universe.

"It was just nice to know that something we created and touched circled the Earth," says Judy. "Not many people can say that."

LUCY

RICK AND CHARLIE

HAZEL AND JENNIFER

The Buffalo Girl Café?

Happy National Bison Day. How did you celebrate?

It's November 2, 2013, and I'm glued to my laptop in Toronto, Ontario, finishing this adventure cookbook on the second annual National Bison Day.

Okay, so the day is an American thing, not a Canadian thing. But it's official. The United States Senate just unanimously passed a resolution that recognizes bison for shaping America's history, economy, culture, and landscape.

The Vote Bison coalition made it happen. The grassroots movement is still lobbying to have the plains bison declared America's national mammal. It's already the mammal of three states, and its image is all over flags, coins, official seals, and logos.

There's one sentence on the coalition's website, votebison.org, that resonates with me. It explains in 13 words why bison are so captivating: "In bison, we recognize aspects of our character like fortitude, boldness, and independence." I like to think of myself as bold and independent, so there's definitely some bison in me.

I'd love to be in Rapid City, South Dakota, right now. There's a National Bison Day celebration at the Museum of the American Bison. But Rick's at the ranch tagging calves, and I'm in Toronto with the kids musing about whether Canada should also give bison a celebratory day and symbolic status.

We already have two national mammals—the beaver (which makes sense) and the Canadian horse (who knew?). "Friendly Manitoba" considers bison its official symbol and puts it in the top-right corner of every license plate. Canada Post occasionally puts bison on stamps. And I have a $10 silver coin featuring a wood bison from the Royal Canadian Mint. Rick had it turned into a necklace and gave it to me for Christmas one year.

I haven't written much about the wood bison, which is a threatened species that's bigger and darker than the plains bison and has a more pronounced hump. Canada used to have nearly 200,000 of them, but they neared extinction in the early 1900s because of overhunting and human encroachment. Parks Canada helped save them. There are now more than 10,000 of them in the wild, mainly in Wood Buffalo and Elk

Island National Parks. There are also some pure wood bison, as well as wood/plains crosses, in private herds.

"Long an example of humanity's destructive power, the bison has, for far longer, been a Canadian icon, symbol of the West, and a core component of the pantheon of Canadiana," writes the Royal Canadian Mint. Powerful words. Who wouldn't want to help this resilient giant?

I'm inspired by Michelle Young, a single mother who is cutting her way through the red tape to create the first private bison herd in Newfoundland and Labrador with 15 wood bison. She wanted a low-maintenance, nontraditional animal and healthy meat for her JNJ Bison Company.

Me, I'm toying with the idea of quitting my high-profile, big-city food-writing job and moving to the ranch for good. Am I tough enough to do manual labor and become a bison rancher instead of a bison rancher's wife? Should I take over meat sales and start selling our bison at farmers' markets and to chefs across Canada? Or is my niche teaching the world how to cook bison?

I've been collecting ideas.

Buffalo Horn Ranch near Calgary, Alberta, has an annual customer appreciation day called Buffalo Mother's Day. Customers get to see cows frolic with their calves, and enjoy a bison burger barbecue and ranch tour. In Quebec, La Terre des Bisons has bison and elk on its 400 acres (160 hectares) and offers family-friendly guided tours, wagon rides, tastings, a boutique, and the chance to meet a domesticated bison named Buffy.

Our ranch is probably too remote and too large, and our bison too wild, to embrace agritourism this way. I'd love to find homes for all our animal parts though. Bison hides can be tanned and turned into all kinds of things. In Alberta, rancher Adele Boucher is exploring ways to collect the bison hair from the hide. Sylvie Toupin runs Fibre-Isle on Prince Edward Island making bison yarn. Bison leather is used to make purses, briefcases, wallets, boots, gloves, and furniture. We've tanned a few of our hides into "robes" (I'd call them rugs but they can be used as wall hangings or bedcovers) with tawny to chocolate brown hair. We sell mounted heads and sun-bleached skulls.

I took a road trip to the Little Ghost Town on the Prairie (littleghosttown.com) to pick up a couple of the robes that we'd been trying to sell on consignment but needed

LITTLE GHOST TOWN ON THE PRAIRIE

back for a silent auction. It's an antiques/ice cream store in Del Bonita, a hamlet near an Alberta/Montana border crossing with a population of next to nothing. But one of those people is Joanne McLeay, who is refurbishing a collection of pioneer stores that she bought for a song on her Visa card more than a decade ago. Like the bison, she is bold and independent and clearly has a tough spirit. I treat myself to a kitschy buffalo-shaped Avon cologne bottle from the 1960s and a saskatoon berry ice cream cone.

Joanne inspires me. She reminds me that what I really want to do is open a coffee shop with a corner devoted to bison curios and freezer sales (a popular way to sell meat in these parts). People could hang out over great coffee, espresso, and tea, and I would feed them baked goods and something made with bison every day.

I would call it the Buffalo Girl Café.

Measurement Conversion Charts

VOLUME	
¼ tsp	1 mL
½ tsp	2 mL
¾ tsp	4 mL
1 tsp	5 mL
1 Tbsp	15 mL
1½ Tbsp	22.5 mL
4 Tbsp = ¼ cup	60 mL
⅓ cup	75 mL
½ cup	125 mL
⅔ cup	150 mL
¾ cup	175 mL
1 cup	250 mL
2 cups	500 mL
3 cups	750 mL
4 cups	1 L
5 cups	1.25 L
6 cups	1.5 L
8 cups	2 L

WEIGHT	
1 oz	30 g
2 oz	60 g
3½ oz	100 g
¼ lb = 4 oz	115 g
5 oz	140 g
6 oz	170 g
½ lb = 8 oz	225 g
¾ lb = 12 oz	340 g
14 oz	397 g
1 lb = 16 oz	450 g
1¼ lb	565 g
1½ lb	680 g
2 lb	900 g
3 lb	1.3 kg
4 lb	1.8 kg
4½ lb	2 kg
5 lb	2.3 kg
6 lb	2.7 kg
7 lb	3.2 kg
8 lb	3.6 kg

CANS AND BOTTLES	
4 oz	114 mL
5½ oz	156 mL
11½ oz	341 mL
14 oz	398 mL
19 oz	540 mL
25.4 oz	750 mL
28 oz	796 mL

OVEN TEMPERATURES	
170°F	77°C
200°F	100°C
225°F	105°C
250°F	120°C
275°F	135°C
300°F	150°C
325°F	160°C
350°F	180°C
375°F	190°C
385°F	195°C
400°F	200°C
415°F	210°C
425°F	220°C
450°F	230°C
500°F	260°C

MEAT COOKING TEMPERATURES		
Roasts		
Rare – cook to	125°F	52°C
Rare – after resting	135°F	57°C
Medium-rare – cook to	135°F	57°C
Medium-rare – after resting	145°F	63°C
Medium – cook to	145°F	63°C
Medium – after resting	155°F	68°C
Steaks		
Rare – cook to	130°F	54°C
Rare – after resting	135°F	57°C
Medium-rare – cook to	140°F	60°C
Medium-rare – after resting	145°F	63°C
Medium – cook to	150°F	66°C
Medium – after resting	155°F	68°C
Ground meat + sausages		
Cook to	160°F	71°C

PANS	
9 × 5 × 3 inches	23 × 13 × 8 cm
13 × 9 inches	33 × 23 cm

LENGTH	
¼ inch	6 mm
½ inch	1 cm
¾ inch	2 cm
1 inch	2.5 cm
1½ inches	4 cm
2 inches	5 cm
2½ inches	6 cm
3 inches	8 cm
4 inches	10 cm
5 inches	13 cm
6 inches	15 cm
8 inches	20 cm
9 inches	23 cm
10 inches	25 cm
12 inches	30 cm
16 inches	41 cm

Index

Acknowledgments

Bringing a cookbook to life is a staggering amount of work. You spend months alone, grocery shopping, cooking, managing leftovers, washing dishes, and writing. But on either side of that solitude are the people who make your book possible.

Ruth Linka made my dream come true on May 21, 2013, when she replied to my pitch with an email saying, "I'm very interested in this project and would like to talk with you more." My stomach still does somersaults reading those words. As publisher of TouchWood Editions, Ruth urged me to let this book come to life naturally. We didn't know if it would be a story with recipes or a cookbook with stories. It became an adventure cookbook just before Ruth moved to Orca Book as associate publisher.

Taryn Boyd jumped in to fill Ruth's shoes as associate publisher of TouchWood and guided this book from manuscript to reality.

A big hug to Robert McCullough (who published my first book, the *Toronto Star Cookbook* at Appetite by Random House) for the matchmaking.

Chicago literary agent Amy Collins and Canadian-turned-Californian writing coach Dianne Jacob helped polish my pitch. Seattle documentary food photographer Clare Barboza was keen to come on a road trip to the ranch, but alas the timing didn't work.

Foremost photographer and teacher Kim Wright came to the ranch twice for photo shoots and managed to make a haggard mom look good.

Toronto photographer Ryan Szulc, food stylist Noah Witenoff, and prop stylist Madeleine Johari do dazzling work. Thanks also to Matthew Gibson (Ryan's assistant) and Amy Webster (Noah's assistant).

The crew at TouchWood was a pleasure to work with. Editor Cailey Cavallin whipped the manuscript (and metric conversions) into shape. Designer Pete Kohut made everything beautiful. Grace Yaginuma handled the proofreading, and Karen Griffiths took on the finicky job of creating the index. Thanks in advance to promotions and marketing assistant Tori Elliott for creating buzz for this book.

I count two people as mentors and moral compasses. Monda Rosenberg knows everything there is to know about food and cooking, and it's a joy to have become friends. Kevin Maclean was my frontline boss at the *Toronto Star* for years. He kept me relatively

calm and steady and provided unlimited advice on everything from journalism and office politics to buying a car. He got inadvertently edited out of the thanks in my last book.

Thank you to everyone who cheered me along this time around—especially Michele Henry, Amy Pataki, Jennifer Wells, Amy Bodman, Megan Ogilvie, Kim Honey, and the parents at Blake Street Public School.

Thank you to the *Toronto Star* for publishing a story about the ranch, "At Home on the Range," on September 26, 2009. I've used a portion of that story, with permission, as the basis for my introduction.

Writing a cookbook eats up your time and energy. Thank you to my kids, Lucy, Hazel, and Charlie, for putting up with my grouchiness; my mom, Barbara, for really coming through with babysitting at crunch time in Toronto; my mother-in-law, Margaret, for babysitting at the ranch; and my brother, Michael, and sister-in-law, Jennifer, for always helping. My husband, Rick, puts up with me, eats everything put in front of him, bakes pies, and raises bison—what more could a woman want?

A shout-out to all of the buffalo (bison) people who helped me, starting with Linda Sautner from the Bison Producers of Alberta, Terry Kremeniuk from the Canadian Bison Association, and Dave Carter from the National Bison Association. These pages are filled with ranchers and chefs who shared their stories and recipes. Please buy their meat and eat in their restaurants.

Finally, thank you to the bison for being so inspiring.

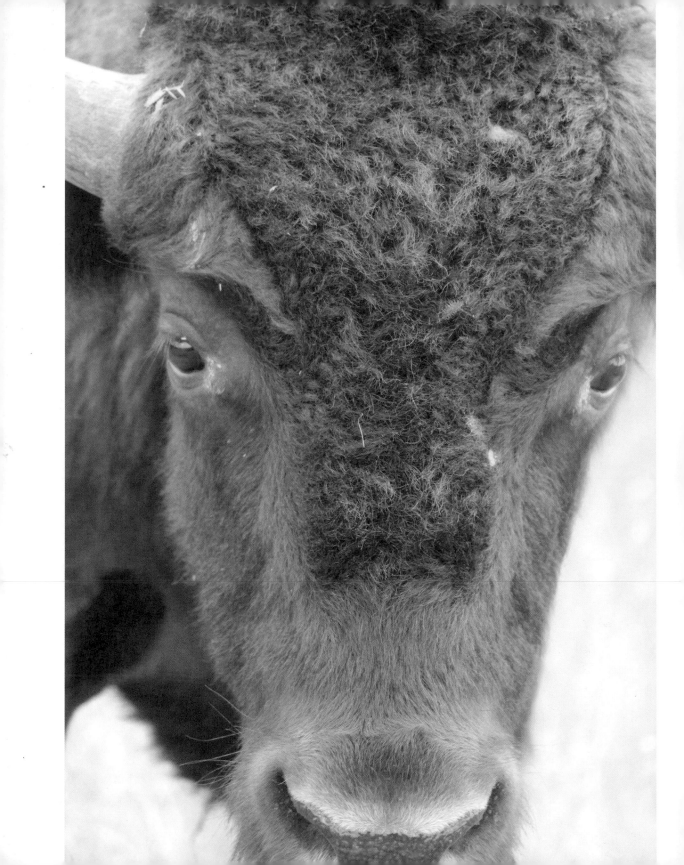